Getting the Very Best
From Your Router

GETTING THE VERY BEST FROM YOUR
ROUTER

PAT WARNER

BETTERWAY BOOKS
CINCINNATI, OHIO

Other fine Betterway Books are available from your local
bookstore or direct from the publisher.

00 99 98 97 96   5 4 3 2 1

Library of Congress Cataloging-in-Publication Data

Warner, Pat.
    Getting the very best from your router / Pat Warner.
        p.   cm.
    Includes index.
    ISBN 1-55870-399-3 (alk. paper)
    1. Routers (Tools) 2. Woodwork. I. Title.
TT203.5W37   1996
684'.083—dc20   96-20180
                                             CIP

Edited by Adam Blake
Content Editing by Bruce Stoker
Production Editing by Michelle Kramer
Interior designed by Brian Roeth
Cover designed by Sandy Kent
Cover photography by Ron Forth Photography

Betterway Books are available for sales promotions, premi-
ums and fund-raising use. Special editions or book excerpts
can also be created to specification. For details contact: Special Sales Manager, F&W Publications, 1507 Dana Avenue,
Cincinnati, Ohio 45207.

DISCLAIMER

To prevent accidents, keep safety in mind while you work. Use the safety guards installed on power equipment; they are for your protection. When working on power equipment, keep fingers away from saw blades, wear safety goggles to prevent injuries from flying wood chips and sawdust, wear ear protection to protect your hearing, and consider installing a dust vacuum to reduce the amount of airborne sawdust in your woodshop. Don't wear loose clothing, such as neckties or shirts with loose sleeves, or jewelry, such as rings, necklaces or bracelets, when working on power equipment, and tie back long hair to prevent it from getting caught in your equipment. People who are sensitive to certain chemicals should check the chemical content of any product before using it. The author and editors who compiled this book have tried to make all the contents as accurate and correct as possible. Plans, illustrations, photographs and text have been carefully checked. All instructions, plans and projects should be carefully read, studied and understood before beginning construction. Due to the variability of local conditions, construction materials, skill levels, etc., neither the author nor Betterway Books assumes any responsibility for any accidents, injuries, damages or other losses incurred resulting from the material presented in this book.

ACKNOWLEDGMENTS

Being confined to only one specialty has led me to believe that perhaps "I know it all." Moreover when I'm stumped, a consultation with the experts is more often disappointing than satisfying. On closer inspection, I think this hornblowing is really just an expression of frustration because I know I will always know less than there is to know about routing.

For their help in producing this book I'd like to thank the following people, in no particular order. Judith A. Warner; John McDonald of *Woodwork*; Pat Spielman; Al and Joan Weiss; Steve Spoon and Rob Ricci of WKW; Jürgen Amtmann for his engineering advice; Bob Clark of Escondido; Jerry Funk; Dennis Huntsman, Leslie Banduch, Julius Boyd, Bob Brown, Robbin L. Massey, Rick Schmidt and Jeff Stoltz of Porter Cable; Sandor Nagyszalancy; Bob Rosendahl; Barry Renstrum and Bill Clark of PRC; Steve Kirby, Dave Thompson, Chris Feddersohn and Russ Filbeck of Palomar College; Eric Johnson; Ralph and Doris Lundvall; Jim Tolpin; Nick Arthur; Charley Robinson; Chuck Masters; Vini Laurence; Jonathan Binzen; Nathan and Trina; Carlo Venditto and Cliff Paddock of CMT Tools; Jane Schlag; Cindy Hughey; Tom Maggard; Joe Kline; Bill Carpenter; Joe Coleman; Martha Botos and Bill Watkins; Kaine Shew; Charlie McGhee; Bob Korn; Jean Miskimon of Eisner & Associates, Inc. representing DeWalt Industrial Tools; John Sherman; David Sellers of *American Woodworker*; Thaddeus Jozefawicz, M.D.; Coyla and Curt Wilson, M.D.; Mike McCue of L.S. Starrett; Fredricka D. Warner; Bob Stevenson of Chula Vista; Phil Stivers; Craig Umanoff; Tom Menard; Cliff Vanderweg; John Goff; Kit Wilson; Eddie Vargas; Peter Wile, M.D.; Robert O. Weisman; Richard Wedler of Microfence; Nan Bushley; Baron Faustin; Hoss Denison; Mel Forman; Dick Erickson; Ron Goldman; and a special thanks to Ken Schroeder of Alliance, Ohio for his outstanding printing of all the photos in this book and his advice to me on just how to shoot film.

ABOUT THE AUTHOR

The clay sculptor has the ideal opportunity to contend with any of his mistakes. The malleability of his material allows for an infinite number of remedies at little expense or risk to the project. The woodworker, on the other hand, has only two choices when presented with an error. He can make the workpiece over or change the work to suit the mishap; both options are likely to involve compromise. The key, then, is getting it right the first time.

My nature is to make mistakes. I'm not one to get it right on the first go-around. Notwithstanding if I do it more than once, I usually do it better each time. Twenty-three years of self-taught woodworking has been one long series of mistakes. However, since I've screwed up so many times in so many ways, I've become pretty good at what I do.

My education was in the sciences and therefore I have learned and I've been blessed with excellent observational skills. This combination of hands-on experience and a keen sense of the task make it easy for me to know when something is apt to go wrong; when I'm in uncharted territory, I'm only half as likely to blow it.

As a furniture designer/craftsman, I've designed and made hundreds of pieces. I'm skilled in case goods and sleepware and I'm no stranger to benches, desks, tables and seating. I've made all my jigs and fixtures and I've made a few on commission. My primary tool has been and still is the router. I use a dozen or so for ordinary work and I often apply them to tasks most woodworkers would find strange or at the very least serendipitous. I do all my joinery with routers, I joint all stock edges on one, and of course, all my template and pattern work is router cut.

I've been called on by the router bit and router manufacturing industry to consult from time to time and I teach routing at the Palomar Community College in San Marcos, California. I am the inventor of the Acrylic Offset Router Sub-Base and I make the accessory for the Porter Cable Corporation. Incidentally my subbase is hand-fabricated with an assortment of twin-pin, table and hand routers using seven different cutters.

My routing experience has been helpful and of some interest to the readers of many current publications including *Fine Woodworking*, *American Woodworker* and *Woodwork* magazines, the last of which I am a contributing editor.

TABLE OF CONTENTS

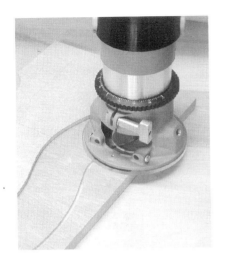

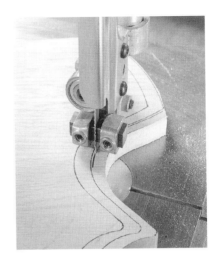

TABLE OF CONTENTS (CONTINUED)

INTRODUCTION

Alot can be said about routing and routers. For example, the router is the second most popular electric hand tool in North America. As of this writing there are at least 87 different fixed and plunge base routers to choose from. Furthermore, with its accessories and cutters, it is often the primary machine and joinery tool in the small shop. It can also be argued that in the right hands, it's capable of more work and diversity than any other woodworking tool.

With an introduction like that you might expect it would take an encyclopedia to describe the router and its uses. And in my view, the subject is simply too diverse to be addressed under one book cover. So, with my experience as a furniture maker and routing instructor, I've narrowed the focus to the more practical and relevant material that will enable you to do a lot of simple things well. This book is for those who are thinking about purchasing a router, and it is also designed for those of you who already rout but are not all that sure of yourself and might like a fresh perspective.

The router is indeed intimidating and, like most power tools, it is dangerous. However, with a good baseline understanding of the tool and its limitations it's a very safe machine. From the literature and from twenty years of personal experience, it is obvious that most accidents are not equipment related—they are almost always due to operator error. Moreover, it is both curious and a fact of woodworking life that safety, skill and quality results are all intimately related.

Because I believe that, and I've written this book with that philosophy, it should be appealing to all woodworkers regardless of skill. After reading *Getting the Very Best From Your Router*, you won't be an ace woodworker—nor will you know all about working wood with a router. You will, however, have a fundamental understanding of just what safe routing is about and the knowledge to proceed and develop your skills confidently and in a practical way.

CHAPTER ONE
The Advantages of Using a Router in Woodworking

Woodworking entirely with hand tools is indeed courageous and noble. The skill required to make an entire piece may take some time to acquire, but for those who have chosen this path, it will no doubt be rewarding. Routing can appreciably shorten the time it takes to do a lot of this hand woodworking. Precision, hand-sawn dovetails, which can take days or weeks to learn and do well, can be mastered in a day or so with a router and templates. Moldings from molding planes, chops from chisels, smooth surfaces from hand jointers and joints from saw joinery tools are everyday simple cuttings with routers. This book is about putting this idea into perspective *and* into practice.

I'd be lying if I said you can walk up to a router, put a bit in the collet and automatically apply the tool correctly in all circumstances. Careful and successful woodworking with a router requires skill, experience and experimentation. Understanding the appropriate use of the tool also requires some general woodworking knowledge.

The possibilities of hand working wood are boundless: Anything is possible—from the shell carvings on breakfronts to the barred glass door joinery of sophisticated china cabinets of the eighteenth century. Router woodworking, on the other hand, has its limitations. Whether you are routing or hand sawing, there are skills to be learned and errors to be made, and lots of practice is required to do the job well. Routing well, however, takes a lot less practice, and if one chooses routing skills over hand skills it will be at the expense of repertoire. Routing should not be considered to have the flexibility of application available to the journeyman joiner or the master hand craftsman. It is, however, a most remarkable invention that has, within its soul and anatomy, more capability than any other single tool.

USING THE ROUTER FOR VARIOUS APPLICATIONS

A router has substantial application potential in joinery, decoration and millwork procedures. Nearly all of the common joints seen in well-made furniture are routable with the appropriate cutters, jigs and fixtures. Tongues and grooves, laps, box joints, dovetails, copes and stickings, glue joints, mortises and tenons, scarfs, splinery and curvy-line complementary joints are all possible with the router (Figure 1-1).

Figure 1-1
These router-cut joinery samples are all possible with hand tools—but they're much easier to learn and do with a router.

Decorative Cutting

Decorative cuttings are probably the most common application of the router. Not only can a workpiece be routed into a more decorative shape, a curved counter top for example, it can be trimmed with any one of hundreds of mold-ings of infinite design range. With single cutters or combinations of cutters set at different depths, you can achieve any number of attractive and professional-looking profiles. Nearly every edge of any element of a piece of furniture or accessory can be trimmed with a decorative cutter. Consider, for example, stiles and rails, drawer fronts, table tops and legs, panels, shelves, pulls and handles, picture frames, doors, door openings, handrails, windows and crown moldings. You can be sure that most of the corners of any workpiece, after the shaping and joinery are complete, can and will be routed, even if it's only to break the edge (Figures 1-2 and 1-3).

Milling With the Router

Router millwork capabilities are just as ambitious and just as important as those of joinery and decoration. My definition of millwork is a little different than that of the lumberyard. Router milling in this instance includes that group of work not directly related to joinery or

Figure 1-2
A router-cut ogee like this one really dresses up a workpiece edge, and you can be good at it with an hour or so of training and practice.

Figure 1-3
The subtle curve along the credenza top and the soft roundover are both hallmarks of dignity in a piece of furniture.

Figure 1-4
The quarter-circle template was cut with the router and circle-cutting base. The notched workpiece is a common router cut.

decoration, but rather to processes like making and using templates, circle cutting, rounding stock for dowels, bowl and tray excavations, wasting operations, threading, notching and jointing (Figure 1-4).

UTILIZING THE ROUTER'S UNIQUE FEATURES

Aside from its application repertoire, the router enjoys special attention because of its unique access to a workpiece and because it is the champion of jig and fixture accessories. Let me explain. A band saw, aside from a rewelded blade, must begin its work from the edge of stock; a table saw has the same problem. Jointers, planers and so on all have their difficulties in approaching a workpiece. A router, on the other hand, within limits, can begin its cut almost anywhere. It's possible, for example, to enter and cut anywhere blindly, or completely through the face of a workpiece, never approaching or cutting through an edge. A template can assist in such a task, but it is not essential. The edge or end grain of a workpiece can be stop or through cut with the workpiece on edge, on face or on end. You'd be hard pressed to find any single electric tool that can do that. Some of the router's popularity—and clearly its utility—is directly related to this phenomenon.

USING JIGS, FIXTURES AND ACCESSORIES

The router is by far the most indulgent tool with respect to jigs and fixtures, and this aspect of its personality rounds out the reasons the machine is so widely accepted. The router is really a simple tool. Anatomically, it's an armature situated in a set of bearings that spins like mad in an electric field. There is a mechanism, a collet, to hold its cutters and a means for raising or lowering the motor with respect to its base plate—and that's about it. It's because of this simple design that so much stuff is necessary for it to function well.

Most tools, especially stationary ones, are designed and supplied with the essential control and workpiece surfaces and a means for changing cutting tool locations. Radial, band and table saws, for instance, all come supplied with large work surfaces, fences, guards and the hardware to position the blade or table. Almost nothing extra is required for these tools to slot, rip, x-cut, dado, tongue, groove or otherwise perform their natural functions (Figure 1-5).

The router is at sea without accessories. There is virtually no way to control it without buying or making something to do so (see chapter four). The router is like the gold razor without blades. The blades in this case are the accessories, hardware and cutters. This is great if you like the details of the project as much as the project itself, and perhaps not so great if the project is of primary importance. Regardless of your interpretation, routing is a challenge—perhaps so much so that this aspect alone will offset the at-tention-to-detail idiosyncracy I just mentioned.

To illustrate, let me cite a few examples. Of the eighteen routers I use, seven use different sets of wrenches and twelve use different collet designs. Two of the routers use the same edge guide, while the others each use different hardware to secure and travel. Some of the guides are metric, others English. The base plates and castings are different in seventeen of the eighteen samples. The mechanisms to raise and lower the motors are just as variable: In several cases the motor is hung on a ring (Milwaukee); another uses an external spiral ramp (Bosch); still another uses a rack and pinion (B&D); and Porter Cable uses a captured pin-in helix configuration. Plunge routers use a different concept that renders the motor essentially inseparable from the rest of the router casting. These motors bounce on spring-loaded hardened tubes. Now all this variability is wrought, on one hand, with irksome attention to detail; on the other hand, if you know your stuff well and you're organized, you can exploit these differences for the best cutting results.

Figure 1-5
This assortment of wrenches, bearings, collars and cutters is just a fraction of my router "stuff" inventory.

Figure 1-6A

Figure 1-6A
This cross cut is referred to several times in this book. It is an important router operation you should know about and practice.

Figure 1-6B
I've matched the cutter and the router to its setup. Look at how clean the cut is when you pay attention to the details.

PAYING ATTENTION TO THE DETAILS

So much for identifying the hardware. Let me illustrate now with a procedure. For example, I'd like a ½″ wide by ¼″ deep through dado in roughly the middle of a board. Now, I know this is a power-hungry operation since the cutter will not only be cutting both sides of the slot, it'll also be cutting on the bottom—and all in one pass. I'll need at least 1½ hp if the cutter is sharp. I have a right-angle template that will assist in the cut, and it should be calibrated regularly. A collar guide can and will be used, so I've got to pick one out of my inventory of a dozen or so. I'll use my offset subbase for flatness and control. The cut is single depth; I don't need the rapid multidepth capability of the plunge router, so my decision is to use a fixed-base tool. The depth of cut is critical in this case and the best fixed-base depth control can be found on Porter Cable models 7518 and 7519, so that's what I'll use. After I select the cutter, insert it and tighten it in the collet, I have to fasten the collar guide and set the depth of cut. The location of the template is next and I must consider a certain offset from its exact location on the workpiece because the collar and cutter are different diameters. I hope you're getting the picture. The devil is in the details alright, but I hasten to add that, if the cut were to be done on the table saw, layout, fence settings, stock preparation, blade height and selection are also details (and decisions) that have to be attended to. I admit, more attention is required in the routing approach, but in my view, at very low risk to the worker and workpiece, a perfect or near-perfect result is ensured (Figure 1-6).

Routing, like any other art, cannot be learned in a day nor can it be expected to be the quick-fix "silver bullet" we're all looking for. Routing is a very exacting woodworking process that will take some time and practice to get used to. Looking at the whole picture (a shell-carved block front for example) can be overwhelming; but if taken in steps as in the upcoming chapters, woodworking with the router will be enjoyable and predictable and will perhaps become your primary means of furniture and cabinet making (Figure 1-7).

TYPES OF ROUTING

Now that we have an overview of just what can be done with a router, let's look at the different types of routing and which routers are appropriate for each application. The categories are trim, table, template, plunge and production routing.

Figure 1-7
This sliding dovetail and the double tongue and groove prove just how close a process routing can be.

Trim Routing

Trim routing is probably the easiest to do, and consequently the most common. Trim routing refers to those easy and low-energy operations performed on the edges of stock (hence "trim"). Typical cuttings may be bevels, small round-overs, rabbets, reliefs, ogees, coves, beads or flutes. The amount of material removed, by my definition, shall be less than ⅜″ square, and the process shall be of short duration. The cuttings are usually and most easily done with bearing-piloted cutters (Figure 1-9) on the stock itself rather than with the aid of a template. Also, the cuttings are to be done with the handheld fixed-base router, a Porter Cable 690 for example, with an offset subbase accessory (Figure 1-8). A plunge router is designed and balanced more for inside (within the perimeter) multidepth cuttings and is therefore not my candidate for these single-depth outside cuts. The power requirements are defined to be about 1½ hp and tool weights are under 10 lbs. If the router is heating up and making a lot of noise and/or the cutter is burning the stock, you're not trim routing—you're in the area I call *production routing*.

Production Routing

Production routing is a rather loose term I use to describe those cuttings that are also outside and single depth, often template assisted and where the waste is greater than ⅜″ square. The duty cycle is long and may last all day. It is trim routing on a much larger scale. You may not be in an actual production shop environment but the cuttings require the likes of a production tool like the fixed-base Porter Cable model 7518 3¼ hp router—2½ hp will do but 3 hp is better. The cuttings can be done with the plunge router and there are plenty of 3 hp production plunge routers around. But in my view, the best power-

Figure 1-8

A 1½ hp Porter Cable router at work on the long-grain edge of a workpiece. Trim routing is the most common of all routing procedures.

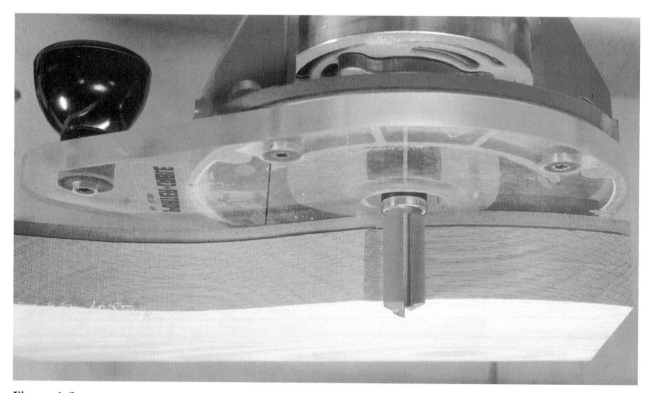

Figure 1-9

All-day template routing the full thickness of a workpiece requires a lot of power. Control and handling are also important factors in quality work.

to-weight ratio and best handling characteristics of any router in this heavy-duty class is the Porter Cable 7518, again using the offset subbase accessory. Taking a lot of material for a long time from the edges and ends of stock is difficult work, and handling, control and power, in that order, are the prime ingredients for consistent and high-quality results.

I would like to emphasize this handling and control issue a bit further, both from the safety and the end-result perspectives. Fixed-base routers have round bases; cuttings along the edges of stock leave less than half of the base plate on the work surface. As you navigate the corner turn on rectangles and squares, less than ¼ of the plate is on the substrate (¼ of the disk). Most plunge router base castings are little more than semicircles, so when cutting outside long-grain profiles there is even less casting surface to

work surface contact than with a round base. Moreover, when routing around the corners with a plunge router there is so little footprint on the work surface that it's nearly impossible to rout effectively (Figure 1-10). Safety is compromised, burning is common, and torn grain and kickback can and will occur. A properly designed offset subbase on the fixed-base router will prevent this from happening. Porter Cable's pre-machined offset subbases on their tools are the best and safest to use, and their unique close-quartered design allows for complete, safe, unencumbered circumnavigation of most workpieces without any loss of control. Try as you like—and as I did—you'll never get complete control on outside cuts without one of these plates. Use a Porter Cable subbase, or at the very least consider making your own from fiberboard, plywood or clear plastic.

Figure 1-10
Note how little of the round base plate (left) is on the work at the end of the cut. Compare that to the offset plate. The offset plate also allows palm pressure directly on the work surface so that you can control the router throughout the corner turn.

Plunge Routing

Plunge routing is a rather limited but important manner of routing. Before the introduction of the plunge router, certain routing processes were not only risky but really quite difficult to do. The cuts I'm referring to are any of those inside cuts that require the cutter to be extended with the router off the substrate to start the cut. (You can't safely start a router with the extended cutter resting on the work surface. Edge cuts can and should begin with the cutter extended to full depth, but on start-up be sure the cutter is at least one cutter diameter away from the edge.) Mortises in particular were quite skill dependent for me because not only did I have to aim the powered bit at the mortise site, I had to change the depth under power in the mortise. Any blind inside excavation done with a fixed-base router was and is a safety hazard. Moreover, it is harder on bearings and cutters than any other operation. Note, however, that if the excavation has access to any edge then it is not blind and the cutter can enter via the edge quite safely. It's the blind cuts that are scary but the total and safe domain of the plunge router (Figure 1-11).

Incidentally, the evolution of router sales has been such that more plunge routers are being sold today than fixed-base tools, and they're used for all types of routing. For me, however, their real strengths are in handheld multistage routings primarily away from the outside perimeter of the workpiece. (For an in-depth look at the plunge router, see chapter three.)

Table Routing

Table routing, in most cases, is done with the router inverted, fastened to a flat work surface and mounted on a stand. At least 80 percent of handheld router operations can be done on the router table. There are a lot of advantages to its use, but the most conspicuous is its efficiency. It is often just easier and safer to cut on the table than it is to cut by hand. I do most straight-line edge work on the table and most of the curvy

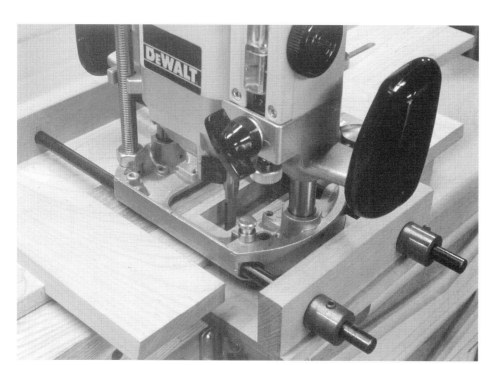

Figure 1-11
The plunge router is "at home" when it's well supported by jig and/or workpiece. A good jig (unfortunately mostly covered up by this router) is critically related to the outcome of your work.

stuff by hand. I also recommend that large cutters, greater than 1¾″ in diameter, should only be used on a table (Figure 1-12).

The safe workpiece feed direction on the router table is into the cutter rotation (right to left as you face the work side of the fence). As a consequence the cutter pulls the stock to the fence and takes a full profile instantly. This is not necessarily the case with the handheld router, and therefore, in general, table routing requires more horsepower than the handheld tool. It is also because of this that production and other heavy-duty work is most often done on the table.

The router table is indispensable in routing, but it does require some precision and care to make one, whereas the handheld router is ready for work right out of the box. A fixed-base router is the best choice of casting and motor in the table, and the bigger the better. (For reasons a plunge router is not recommended for table use, see chapter nine.) Experimental work and template routing take more setup and sophistication on the table; I do most of these cuttings portably.

Template Routing

Templates are patterns or forms that are fastened to and copied onto the workpiece. A template system requires either the use of a bearing-guided cutter or template guide collar to follow the pattern. The cutting edges of the router bit should never touch the template. Template work integrates all the other types of routing either in the creation of the template itself or in its use. Routings can be blind, ½ blind, full or fractional thickness, inside or out. A plunge router can often be used, and in production routing the table is often the best choice.

A template is really software. It has enough

Figure 1-12
I designed this large-diameter 45° cutter for some experiments. I need the fence of the router table for a safe and well-controlled cut. The chamber behind the cutter is exhausted for obvious reasons.

information encoded on it to form a workpiece in nearly any configuration on flat material. Spherical surfaces, however, are extremely difficult to fixture and are best rendered pantographically. Any router can be used to template rout, and the same template can be used with different tooling or intent to produce a variety of different routings—a truly amazing and serendipitous discovery (Figure 1-13).

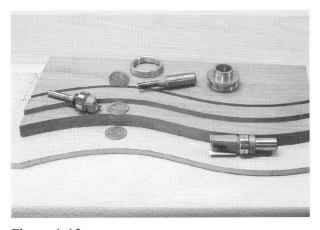

Figure 1-13
This workpiece was template routed with the same template in three different modes. First it was thickness routed, then line cut, and finally a cut was made at half depth.

CHAPTER TWO
The Fixed-Base Router

The term *fixed-base* refers to the design and non-plunging action of these routers. A plunge router's depth-adjusting system allows for rapid and instant depth-of-cut changes under power or with the motor off. The fixed-base tools are also designed for easy depth changes, but not with the motor running. The depths of cut are set prior to the cutting procedure and by nature are "fixed" and generally used only at one depth for a given cut; dovetails, ogees or rabbets, for example. (Figure 2-1)

FIXED-BASE ANATOMY

There are maybe thirty-five or so different fixed-base routers that all share the same anatomy, namely a separate cylindrical base casting and a motor. Most of these motors can be pulled from their bases for easy cutter changes or template collar guide fixturing. There are four different methods of raising and lowering the motors in these tools and each has its advantages.

Different Types of Height Adjustment
The Helical Ramp
The Bosch system uses an outside helical ramp on the casting. The motor has a pointer projec-

Figure 2-1
This heavy-duty fixed-base router is an excellent tool for most routing procedures, including router table work.

tion that slides up and down the ramp. Of all the systems this one is the least accurate, but it is very easy to use. There is no machine backlash

Figure 2-2

A Bosch 1604. The measured travel is only about an 1⅛". I filed away the pointer for a little more motor travel. (You are cautioned that any modification to a router may null its warranty or present a safety hazard.)

The Rack and Pinion

The rack and pinion system is used on some Sears tools and the DeWalt 610, a commercially rated tool. The tool has ample vertical travel with the rack and it is zeroable at any point in its travel. You can start at zero or any fraction of an inch. Depth settings are easy, accurate and precise, though the calibrated knob is difficult to read. A white or yellow marking wax can be worked into the reference marks for easy viewing, however. The action is continuous and relatively smooth. The pinion gear, journaled in a strap of the casting, also provides a means for locking the motor. For more comfort and insurance against an accidental depth-of-cut change, I replaced the locking wing nut with a lever. The lever can be adjusted in any of twelve positions, never interfering with the body casting (Figure 2-3).

Figure 2-3

The DeWalt casting is equipped with a rack and pinion to adjust the motor height. The wing nut has been replaced with an adjustable lever. A "strap" of the casting offers sufficient grip on the motor to lock it at depth.

to contend with and there are no interruptions. The motor ride, up or down the ramp, is smooth throughout the travel limit. The slope is gentle enough that small changes in depth are possible (less than 1/64"). This tool cannot be zeroed, which means you have to take depth readings as they come. You could just as well start at 3/32" or 9/32"—there's no way to start at zero. The mechanism does not function well upside down. Though the relative travel is short, about 1⅛", and the casting is crude, I like the mechanism and recommend it (Figure 2-2).

The Ring-Hung Motor

The ring-hung motor is another usually non-zeroable mechanism for raising or lowering the motor. The mechanism is popular and is used on Milwaukee, Sears and large Bosch tools, as well as on some Japanese imports. The motor barrel on these tools has an external ground spiral (a thread) that engages a plastic ring. The ring rests on the top of the base casting. With the motor clamp loose, you turn the ring in either direction to raise or lower the motor. The mechanism is essentially inactive if the base casting is mounted upside down, as in a router table. With the router upright the mechanism is active through-out the entire travel; the ring can be removed if more travel (equal to the width of the ring) is required. The action is smooth and continuous, with little backlash, and I like it. However, the inability to zero the tool is often enough to persuade me to use the Porter Cable pin-and-helix system tools (Figure 2-4).

The Pin and Helix Design

In this system (now used only by Porter Cable), the motor barrel is studded with four pins that engage a double spiral within the casting. As you rotate the motor, the pins ride up or down the helical ramps, thus raising or lowering the

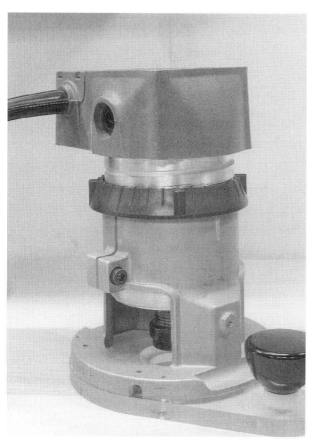

Figure 2-4
The Milwaukee 5680, a 2 hp tool, uses the ring-hung design to effect its motor travel. Note the large flat top and the out of the way wire set. This makes bit changes easier. The mechanism is non-zeroable.

Figure 2-5
The Porter Cable motor is trapped (engaged) in the casting by its pins. This system works while upside down, sideways or right side up. The motor clamp has to be in play for operations. This commercial tool is the best seller in its class in America. The reference-depth ring allows for a start at zero or any fraction of an inch.

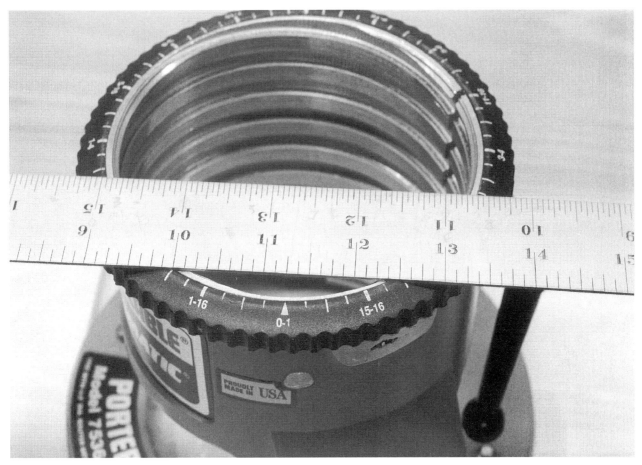

Figure 2-6

This larger Porter Cable base casting has a very conspicuous depth-reference ring. Each mark indicates a ¹⁄₆₄″ depth-of-cut change and they are about ¼″ from one another.

motor. Since the motor is trapped by the pins, it won't fall from the casting when upside down. Therefore, the system is active upside down, sideways or right side up, making it my first choice for router table use (Figure 2-5).

The system is zeroable at any point in its travel. These Porter Cable routers use a calibrated ring for reference and each mark is ¹⁄₆₄″ (Figure 2-6). On their larger tools (2½ hp or more) one motor revolution in the casting (model 7518 for example) is equivalent to 1.00 inch of vertical travel. The mechanism is the most accurate of any router—I often can set the depth of cut to within .002″ of the ring readout.

Dovetails, laps, sticking and other joints demand this kind of accuracy for a good fit.

The system is smooth and continuous, but can be rough as the pins pass by the split in the base casting. If you dust out the spirals regularly, this problem can be kept to a minimum. Moreover, gently supporting the motor as you adjust the depth, thus taking the weight load off the pins, can also smooth out these irregularities.

Motor Locks

For a fixed-base router to function its motor must be locked firmly in the base casting. There

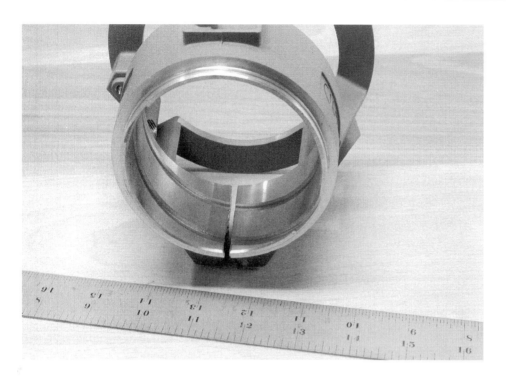

Figure 2-7 & 2-8

The sawn-through split casting (above) allows for a more uniform grip on the motor than the narrow strap (right), which concentrates the grip on the smaller area of the motor housing.

are essentially two different mechanisms to effect this. The least popular one uses a brake pad and studded knob screw that jams the motor against the inside of the casting. In the other system the casting is sawn clear through and a bolt-and-nut assembly pulls the casting tightly and uniformly around the motor. The whole casting squeezes down on the motor. While the Bosch 1604 and the DeWalt 610 use only a strap of the casting—a split-casting hybrid—the mechanisms work well (Figures 2-7 and 2-8).

Motor Clamp Hardware

All fixed-base motors use wing nuts or small threaded clamp knobs to secure the motor clamp. Though they do their job as engineered, I don't trust them and they're all uncomfortable. Furthermore, an unexpected change in depth of cut can often be traced to a loose motor. To ensure against this calamity I've changed all the motor clamp hardware on my routers to Allen-driven cap screws and nuts or adjustable clamp levers. I must caution you, however, should you decide likewise, that changing the hardware will null your warranty. For engineering purposes, if you do decide to change the hardware do not drill out or otherwise alter the casting to accept your fasteners (Figures 2-9 and 2-10).

THE USES OF A FIXED-BASE ROUTER

The fixed-base router works best and most safely on outside cuts or on inside cuts where the cutter can enter from the edge or end of the stock. Plunging a spinning extended cutter down into a workpiece is not safe for the worker or

Figure 2-9
An alloy steel cap screw and nut are my preference for a motor clamp fastener.

Figure 2-10
A lever is easier and more effective than the wing nut that is usually supplied. This lever (supplied by the Reid Tool Co.) is expensive but attractive, comfortable and effective.

Figure 2-11
A bearing-guided outside cut is probably the most frequent and easiest cut to be done with a fixed-base tool.

the work with a fixed-base router. The short horizontal axis of fixed-base routers and their relatively close and low grips make these tools safer on outside cuts than plunge routers. In addition, outside cuts are done most frequently in one pass, and therefore the rapid, multidepth, retractile bit capability of the plunge machine goes unused. Any cutter with a bearing on it can be used on the outside of the stock or template, and consequently is best used in a fixed-base tool (Figure 2-11).

FIXED BASE ADVANTAGES
Easy Motor Separation

A major advantage of a fixed-base tool is cutter access. Most fixed-base motors can be pulled quickly from their castings to facilitate cutter changes. If you do a lot of cutting with many

cutters and only one router, you'll save time and probably do less wrench damage to your cutters using a fixed-base router.

Experimental and Pretest Work

Experimental, template and curvy-line work are best done with fixed-base tools. Most of the cuts that fall into this category are single depth and typically outside; for example, the testing of various roundovers and bevel depths, or the making and use of templates.

End Operations

Many end operations done on the router table with the workpiece held vertically or in a miter gauge are done more accurately and safely with the fixed-base router (Figures 2-12 and 2-13).

Fixtured Work

Both table and hand routing require fixturing the workpiece or adjusting various fences and jigs. In general, the router table is easier to fixture for a cut than fixturing for the same cut to be hand routed, and therefore the job is done more often on the table. There are some cuttings, however, that are best done by hand; if they are done on the router table they're done at some risk and the cuttings are often torn or of inferior quality. Fixturing for the hand router is more difficult to make, but the cutting results are better and less skill is required to do the cutting; there is always a trade-off.

Template Routing

Template work, especially experimental "outside" template work, is by far more expeditious with the fixed-base tool. Templates can be quickly positioned to scribe lines and points along the top side of a workpiece. Clamping

Figure 2-12
End routing a small workpiece on the router table is easy. But getting a good result is another matter. The work is not well supported or backed up. It's sure to tear out and perhaps rock as it passes the cutter.

Figure 2-13
The same cut as in Figure 2-12, but done with the workpiece fixtured. The router is stable with the offset subbase, the work is secured with a clamp and indexed with a fence. End cutting like this is a very low-energy cut and the climb cut (a cut in the direction of the cutter) is permissible here. The climb cut often produces tear-out-free cuttings like this one.

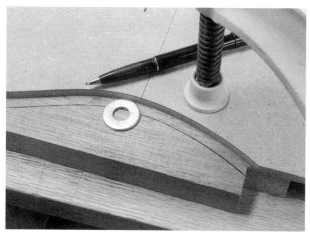

Figure 2-14

This template is easily secured to the workpiece with clamps (at least two at all times). I can follow the pattern with a washer and pen and translate the pattern away from the template.

down of both template and work is quite visible, easy and fast. You can quickly translate layout lines, judge overhang and size up the jobs in general (Figure 2-14). Again, these cuts are best done with the fixed-base router because of the single-depth cut demand of these operations and the exemplary control and handling of these tools. Furthermore, offset subbases which virtually ensure perfect outside cutting, are far more ergonomic on fixed-base tools than on plunge routers.

Using an Offset Subbase

Curvy-line work often positions the router base so far out on a workpiece or template projection that the cut cannot be done safely, if at all, without an offset subbase (Figures 2-15 and 2-16). The subbase itself was my approach to expanding my skills as a woodworker. Early in my work I understood the use and making of templates, but I was weak in the actual routing of the patterns. I invariably lost control around corners, I constantly tipped the router on curves and often hung up the base plate when crossing templates or warped sections of template or workpiece. Once I designed the offset subbase, my work improved immeasurably. Even ordinary straight-line work, often quite variable, was now in my control. (See The Woodworker's

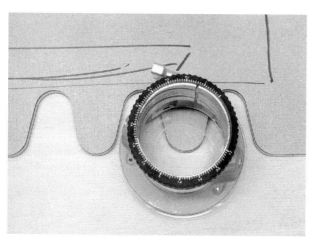

Figure 2-15

The round base is very unstable on this peninsula of the template.

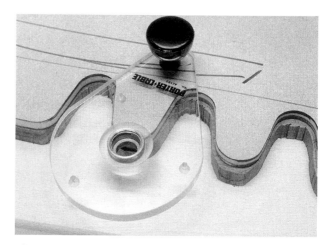

Figure 2-16

The offset subbase can be pivoted around and safely hung an inch or so away from the template. The round base on its casting, with its cutter even ½" from the template, will spell disaster for this job.

Store catalog, or a CMT Tools or Porter Cable dealer for offset subbases.) After an understanding of the work and the equipment to do the work, the handling of the router and its control are paramount. Practice, lots of experimentation and a lot of mistakes will make you a humble and an equally skilled woodworker.

Operations on Wide Stock

Some operations, on panels or glue-ups for example, are often done more expeditiously on the router table. This is acceptable for medium-grade work. However, my experience has shown that router table surfaces and panels are seldom flat enough to be accurately worked on the table. Table cutting on a cupped panel or work surface will be variable. Edge work will show variable depths of cut; inside cuts, already encumbered by a chip that can't escape, will be less than desirable. In these instances, if quality is your goal, use the fixed-base router. Why? Because the panel can be clamped flat and the

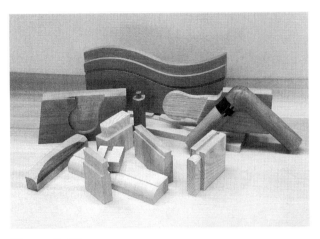

Figure 2-18
An assortment of cuts, all cut with the handheld router.

chip, on inside cuts, can be ricocheted out of the excavation (Figure 2-17).

Decorative panel cuts that play no part in joinery are usually acceptable on the router table, but if the workpiece is to be joined you should use the hand router. Dados, sliding dovetails, laps and end rabbets will all fit their mates more precisely with hand-cut routers. End cuts and miter gauge cuts, often done on narrow stock, will also be more accurate when cut portably with a fixed-base router.

Before closing out this chapter, I'd like to mention the jig/fixture dependence so germane to both the portable plunge and fixed-base routers (See chapter four for more on this). Aside from bearing and template work, with the router on the face of the stock, nearly every hand operation will require a jig or fixture.

As mentioned, generally the router table with its large fence and surface area can be of more use than its portable counterpart without extensive fixturing. Notwithstanding, the jigs for portable router use can be quite simple and fun to use, and will so improve the process that the cuttings will far outclass those produced on the router table (Figure 2-18).

Figure 2-17
The panel here is clamped flat and the 90° template offers a straight edge for the template collar to follow. The cuttings are necessarily messy, but usually quite crisp because the chip is ejected from the slot and the router is up on the template, not on the chip mess below.

CHAPTER THREE
The Plunge Router

The plunge router is a remarkable invention. The plunge router differs from the fixed-base tool primarily by its depth-changing mechanism. Unlike the fixed-base tool, the motor and base castings of the plunger are inseparable. The motor head castings, handles and controls are integrated into a common assembly and placed on a pair of spring-loaded tubes. Since nearly every routing operation is done at a different depth, it makes sense to configure a router for easy, instant and vertical changes in height. The operation of the plunge router is essentially like that of the fixed-base tool—with the exception of the plunging and the instant retraction of the cutter.

The overwhelming percentage of the tool's weight is concentrated in the motor head, which "pogos" on the polished and hardened steel tubes. Unlike the pogo stick, however, the ideal relationship between the base casting and the motor would be one of buoyancy. The pogo stick is designed with a lot of spring resistance to bounce the daylights out of the rider; if a proportionate amount of that overspring was designed into a plunge mechanism, height changes would be difficult. When you select a plunge router, consider one that requires only a moderate force to overcome the springs.

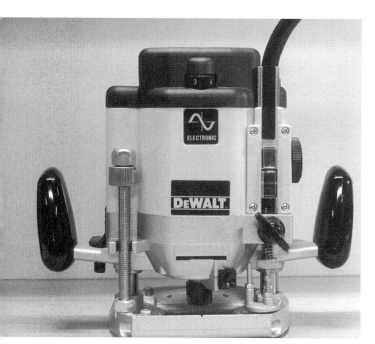

Figure 3-1
This variable speed DeWalt 625 is considered the industry standard in heavy-duty plunge routers.

DEPTH CONTROL

Not surprisingly, most of the features designed into plunge routers are related to depth control. I wouldn't select a router based on these features, however, since they all work about the same. The industry standard is the DeWalt 625, a reliable and powerful router (Figure 3-1). The

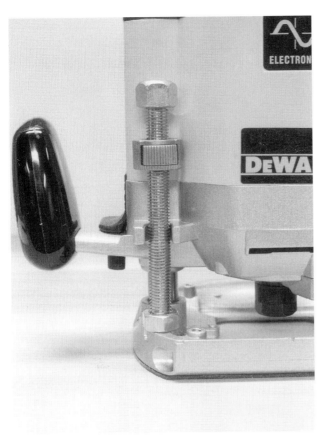

Figure 3-2
The threaded height stop rod and its quick action adjustment nut is located on the operator side of the tool.

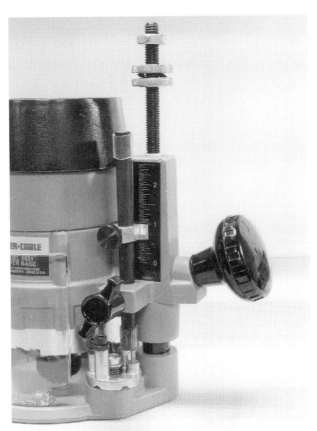

Figure 3-3
The Porter Cable 693 has its height stop rod inside the right casting post.

depth-related mechanisms include the variable height stop, the variable depth stop, the depth turret stop assembly and the motor lock.

The Height Stop

The height stop (Figure 3-2) is a threaded rod with an adjusting nut or nuts that limit the head's upward travel. Some routers have the assembly as a separate entity (as in Figure 3-2) and others integrate the function into one of the guide posts (Figure 3-3). In either case they can facilitate depth adjustment when the motor is unlocked and up against the nuts, much like a drill press stop in reverse. Since the motor (unlocked) is sprung against the nuts, you can advance or retract it by turning the nuts. The mechanism is designed first, however, to be used as the upward

travel limit of the motor head. You should adjust the up stop limit for the cutter to rest up inside the base casting by at least ¼" (Figure 3A). After market fine-adjustment mechanisms are often used in place of the adjuster nuts, especially when the router is used upside down in the router table.

The Depth and Turret Stops

The depth stop is used to limit the downward stroke of the motor travel. In tandem with the adjustable turret stop, this unit can be preset to three different depth positions (Figure 3-4). The intention here is to divide the work up into three near-equal fractions, the total depth usually being impossible in a single pass. Incidentally, herein lies one of the important advantages

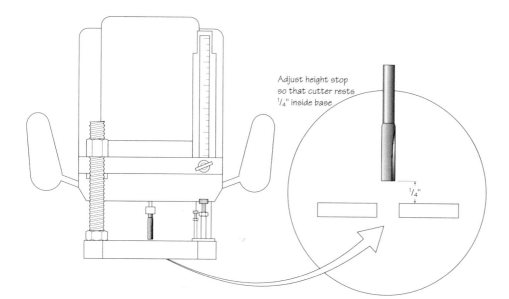

Adjust height stop so that cutter rests ¼" inside base

¼"

of the plunge machine. Since the work can be performed in shallow and quick excavations (routings), not much horsepower is required of a plunge router. A light-duty machine, 1½ to 2 hp, is often all that is required for most plunge router tasks. Single-depth cuts with large diameter bits, frequently more efficiently done with the fixed-base tool, do of course require a lot more power.

The depth stop mechanism on the DeWalt 625 is zeroable because the magnified reader lens can always be set to zero. To use the mechanism, adjust the cutter depth and lock the motor head. Then locate and set the appropriate stud on the turret to coincide with the depth. A spring-loaded fine-adjustment knob is also standard on this tool. The routings are then completed in order, advancing the turret for each depth. Most of the time it is safe to make the depth change under power; adjusting the turret with the motor running, however, is done at some risk. Safe routing requires both hands on the grips—when one hand is on the turret there is a momentary loss of control.

THE MOTOR LOCK

The motor locks on all plunge routers lock up only one side of the tool—only one plunge column is locked. You might think this is insufficient, but it's not. Though you can push down on the motor head with the lock in play and some downward motion is detectable, there is never any vertical-axis force of any appreciable magnitude during a router operation. That is to say, it doesn't matter if only one column is locked up, the tools work fine.

Figure 3-4
The DeWalt depth stop turret has three positions, the Porter Cable has six.

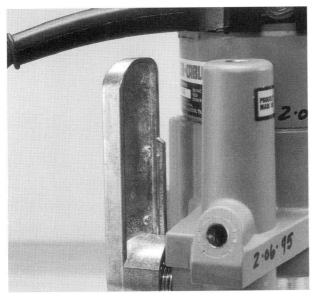

Figure 3-5
Note the spring inside the lever on the Porter Cable plunge. The motor can only be plunged when you activate the lever; the motor head is otherwise always locked to the post (unattended).

There are essentially only two locking lever types among the various plunge routers. The spring-loaded lock is spring loaded in the locked position (Figure 3-5). Therefore, locking the motor head is automatic. Release the lever and the motor locks. The unsprung lock requires you to tighten the lever. Like a nut on a bolt you must tighten it to secure it. It follows then that the spring-loaded lever requires no thought to lock, it's automatic like a self-closing door. The unsprung lock design, if not locked, allows the motor to rise to the upper stop (since all plunge router motor heads are spring loaded to rise). If the motor is up against the upper stop, the cutter is out of play as explained on pages 38-39.

BASE CASTINGS

Plunge router base castings are usually shaped about like a ⅔ semicircle (Figure 3-6). A few have two straight edges with the ends serving as radii and some are round. Since, in my view, the plunge router's playground is away from the perimeter (inside cuts), the shape of the base is unrelated to its performance. If the plunge router is going to be your only router, however, I would suggest the largest round bottom casting available, as this will afford you more stability on outside cuts.

HANDLING AND CONTROL

The electric router evolved as a means to expedite and replace those hand operations done

Figure 3-6
The DeWalt casting is about 70 percent of a 6⅝" semicircle. The production Porter Cable router is a 7" circle.

with hand planes and chisels. One of the reasons hand work could be done so well is the ergonomics of the tool. The chisel or plane is always light in hand, and its weight is never much of an influence with respect to its control. The control lies in the hand and mind of the operator. You will not tire or lose balance due to the weight of the hand tool. To a large measure the basic cutting results are not dependent on the design of the tool, either. The quality of the work, though, is quite clearly related to the design and cutting action of the knife, blade or chisel.

The design of the router, and in particular the plunge router, however, is directly related to the cutting result. The ergonomics, comfort, weight, size and center of mass are essential and critical elements with respect to the quality of the cut. The fixed-base routers, on the one hand, are small, typically under 6″ in diameter, lightweight, and with a low center of gravity. The

hand grips are situated low on the base castings and always in the same place—no matter what depth of cut. All this adds up to reasonable handling and control. The offset subbase makes up for most of what would otherwise be out of our control. The offset knob puts pressure directly down on the substrate, and the tendency to rock or teeter is absent with the knob's use. The influence of the fixed-base router on the cut is manageable, and therefore high-quality results are ensured with only reasonable skill levels, much like the chisel or plane.

The plunge router has sacrificed a lot of this control for the sake of its plunging action. I am reminded of a skit in *Home Improvement* where Tim demonstrates the use of a 3 hp plunge router to his family's dismay. He starts the tool and off it goes with him trailing behind, producing nothing but an accidental pathway through his workpiece.

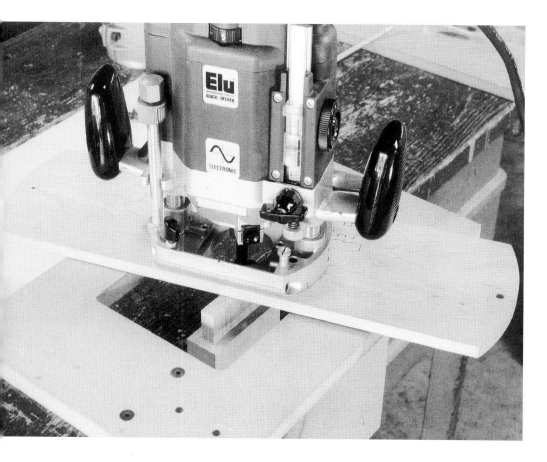

Figure 3-7
This plunge router is mounted on a wide board to prevent it from falling through the window in this tenon-making fixture.

Figure 3-8

Safe edge work is possible when the outward side of the plunge router is supported by material with its thickness equal to the thickness of the workpiece.

Plunge routing is really not difficult if confined to those areas where its base casting is nearly or entirely surrounded by template, substrate or fixture. Edge work, however, is complicated by the ever-changing height of the handles, the higher the handles the less control. It is further aggravated by the unusually wide and high location of the grips, typically 10″ to 13″ apart, and 3½″ to 5″ or more from the work surface, depending on the depth of cut. Moreover, the shape of the base castings is such that the "footprint" on edges and around corners is precariously stingy. Not surprisingly, plunging on the edge of stock without tipping will take some practice; try to confine the use of the plunge router to inside work, or develop strategies where you can get uniform base support (Figures 3-7 and 3-8).

The best jobs for plunge routers are multi-depth operations like mortises, bowl and tray excavations, half laps and similar flat joints, operations where a large ski can be used for support (Figure 3-9), or any job where the cut is not along the perimeter of the workpiece.

FINDING DEPTH

The plunge router excels at "finding depth" better than a fixed-base router. If a surface needs excavation or re-excavation, it's very easy to lightly plunge to that surface (motor off) and "feel" the cutter surface contact, establish depth, lock and rout as necessary. This sensitive tactile interplay with the operator is more difficult with the fixed-base tool.

Figure 3-9

The mortise is a very demanding woodworking chore. The plunge router can carve away at the excavation quickly with as little as an ⅛" of waste per pass. This mortiser has the router controlled with edge guide on both sides and an end stop on each end of the mortise. (Shown without motor.)

NOT FOR THE ROUTER TABLE

I'm not in favor of using the plunge router in the router table (except in one instance I'll refer to later). The usual configuration of plunge router to router table employs the open window approach. In this instance a sizable window is cut into the router table surface for a large plastic rectangular subbase fastened to the router. While this may solve the problem of difficult depth and cutter changes under the table (the large base and router can be removed from the table for these tasks), it does nothing to solve the discontinuity and flatness problems that are sure to occur as a result of the window.

Cutting a window into a large surface invariably distorts the surface. If not immediately, then with time, this much material removal from a slab will cup, twist or otherwise contort it. If the surrounding area can be underlaid with beams, all in the same plane, it is possible to flatten the slab by force. However, in practice this is rarely done. Furthermore the discontinuities alluded to earlier still exist, no matter how flat the slab is.

The discontinuities I refer to are those where the plastic insert meets the window and the rabbet (Figure 3-10). If quality work is what you're after, you will find that as your workpiece slides from table surface to the first insert junction there is a little bump. You will also discover that as the workpiece is pressed down over the insert it will bend, which means the depth of cut will vary. Now as the workpiece passes over the next junction it may bump again. A smooth, uninterrupted workpiece trip is essential for quality table work. Nothing—not the fence, not the work surface, not the insert, not the work—can flex. It will with a table insert.

Certainly ten thousand French woodworkers can't all be wrong; there are thousands of tables like this in use today. And I must concede that satisfactory to excellent results are possible, but the potential for problems is enough for me not to use the plunge router in the router table.

The One Exception

Since plunge routers excel in microdepth adjustment, I might consider using one where the final depth of cut is critical. The procedure would have to be one of great importance, or at the very least a production run. In this case, however, I would bolt the whole machine to the underside of the table and not cut a window into the slab. Not only will this tactic preserve the integrity of the slab, but the casting, having been machined flat, will aid in keeping the surface flat. I might even dedicate the table and router to this specialized duty, but I wouldn't use it as a general router table.

The plunge router is an excellent invention, and any busy woodworker should have at least one. Use it on inside cuts where the cutter must be plunged into the work under power, something the fixed-base tool can only do with risk.

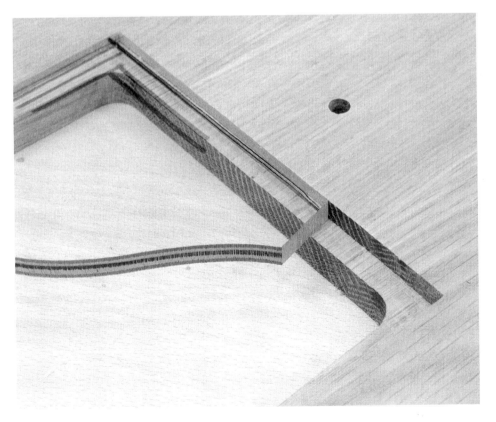

Figure 3-10
The point where the plastic insert meets the rabbet can be problematic. The junction can collect dust, the rabbet must be chip free and the plastic thickness must be exactly equal to the depth of the rabbet. If the insert bends under feed pressure, which is likely, the depth of cut will vary slightly.

Figure 4-8

These are typical bearing/cutter ensembles you can use for a variety of precise cuttings.

ground to a tolerance of a few thousandths of an inch and bearings are ground to tolerances measured in the millionths. Bearings are either on the end of the tool bit or on the shank; either way, they are concentric to the cutting circle. You can count on the cut being directly and uniformly related to the bearing and to the cutting diameters of the tool. If a rabbet bit is 1.000″ in diameter and its bearing is .500″, the rabbet will be .250″ no matter how you navigate the router. If exact predictability is your goal the bearing systems will not fail you. There are problems associated with bearing-guided cuts and cutters, but precision is not one of them (Figure 4-8).

Cutters with bearings require the bearing to engage the workpiece or template for the completion of the cut. Through a clear plastic subbase you can see whether the bearing has reached its target or not. I usually make it a point to cut 80 to 90 percent of the cut before pressing the bearing to the workpiece. It is tricky to keep the bearing from contacting its intended guide edge in an anti-climb cut, but it can be done (see chapter five for more on the direction of feed). In the climb cut, the mode of routing with least tear-out, the bearing is effectively repelled from the work edge—and at some risk, I might add. (The

risk is that on heavy cuts the router tends to run away from the operator, whereas in the left-to-right anti-climb cut the machine resists the feed force and is much more manageable.) In any event, if you can, leave ⅟₃₂″ or so of the cutter profile until the last pass tear-out can be substantially minimized.

Bearings on the End of the Bit

Perhaps half of all router bits are sold with bearings screwed on to the end of the tool. There was a time when these piloted cutters were simply steel rings or bosses that rubbed along the workpiece and often burned themselves and the work. The bearing not only solved the burning problems, but also made routing so much easier that very little skill was necessary for acceptable results.

Almost all operations with end-bearing cutters are outside cuts; that is, on the perimeter of the stock. A few inside cuts are possible if the excavations to be trimmed are deep enough, but generally think of end-bearing cutters as "outside" cutters to be worked on the edges of the stock. There are a few occasions when a template is necessary for an end-bearing cutter to work (Figure 4-9), but most of the time the bearing is riding on the stock itself. End-bearing cutters are most often used to decorate, although rabbetters, flush trimmers and slotters can be used in joinery. Hundreds of different cutters are available with end bearings—they are very common.

Bearings on the Shank

The shank of a cutter is that straight section above the flutes, part of which is held in the collet. Most shanks are long enough that there is room for a bearing and sufficient grip (at least

Figure 4-9

In this instance the full thickness of the sample is being worked. Since the bearing, in practice, is below the workpiece, it must ride on a template. You can trim an edge to a precise 45° at no risk in this setup. Obviously, you must secure the workpiece and template firmly.

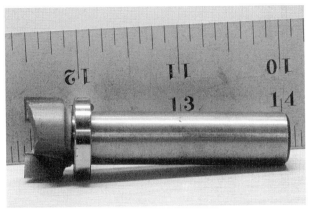

Figure 4-10

The extra-long shank on this CMT cutter has plenty of allowance for a bearing and a safe residence in the collet.

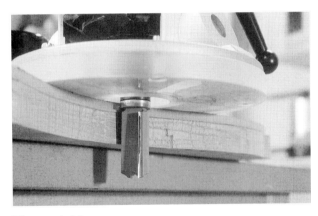

Figure 4-11

Be careful when template routing. In this instance an excess of cutting flute extends beyond the workpiece thickness. The cutter length should be matched as closely as possible to the thickness of the material.

¾″) in the collet (Figure 4-10). In contrast to the end-bearing cutters, almost all shank-bearing cutters need a template to follow. The idea of a template has a built in paradox: Making a template is a relatively difficult task, but on the other hand, using one requires almost no skill at all. The making of the template requires careful design and layout abilities and a multitude of machine and hand skills to do well; the routings are trivial by comparison.

The choices in end-bearing cutters far outnumber shank-bearing cutters. However, most cutters, even end-bearing cutters, will accept bearings on their shanks for special tasks. Ball bearings must contact the template to complete the cut. Once again, a clear plastic subbase will make it easier for you to see when this occurs. Shank-bearing cutters are relatively late in coming to the marketplace, and have not yet reached their full potential.

Since the bearing is above the flute, all of the flute has to be extended below the subbase to expose the bearing to the template (Figure 4-11).

Quite often more flute is extended than necessary, and that can be risky. The flute length of any cutter should match the job. This is not always possible, given our resources, but the principle is an important one in routing. When routing 1″ material in full thickness, for example, the flute length should be no more than 1⅛″. This minimizes deflection and therefore chatter, and with less cutter exposed you are less likely to have an injury.

Shank-bearing-guided cutters also have to

harmonize with the template thickness. A template that's too thick may not allow enough cutter into the stock, and one that's too thin may present too much cutter to the workpiece. Template work is sophisticated and requires attention to a lot of detail. If you are considering a template rout you must take into account the depth of the required cut, the bearing's thickness relationship to the template thickness and the flute lengths of the intended cutters.

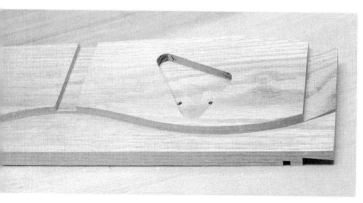

Figure 4-13
This sample has been worked on the end (the dovetail), on the edge (the wavy rabbet) and on the inside (the triangular excavation). The cuttings were all done with shank-bearing cutters and templates.

Most factory-manufactured templates can be used with shank-bearing cutters. The Omnijig, for example, excels at dovetails and box joints (Figure 4-12). Some other typical chores for these cutters include bowl and tray excavations, mortises, jointing and template making. The top-bearing cutters, unlike the bottom bearings, have few restrictions with respect to where they can work. In fact, end, face, inside and edge work are all possible with these tools, either in full or partial thickness (Figure 4-13).

THE TEMPLATE COLLAR GUIDE

Like the shank-mounted bearing cutters, collars afford the router access to any site on a workpiece. A collar acts just like the bearing, but it's attached to the subbase rather than the cutter. The ring and nut assembly (Figure 4-14) is a Porter Cable invention and is considered the industry standard. These accessories can be used directly on the workpiece (Figure 4-15), but invariably are used with templates. They are sup-

Figure 4-14
The Porter Cable subbase here is removed from its casting so you can see just how the collar system is attached.

Figure 4-15
You can, in some instances, use the collar directly on the workpiece, as in this stepped re-excavation for my circle cutter.

plied, like bearings, in many sizes (Figure 4-16), but the threaded section and flange are the same for all of them. The bearing-guided cutters have no cutter sensitivities; a bearing can always be found to fit the shank. Collar use, on the other hand, is restricted to relatively small cutters (less than 1″ in diameter). They are safer than bearing cutters since the correct length of cutter can always be extended. If you are cutting 1″ material, $1\frac{1}{32}$″ cutter extension is all you need, which is a nice advantage.

The collar system does suffer from concentricity problems, and this can be problematic in close work. For general routing, collar systems are quite satisfactory. However, there are at least six areas where router manufacturing tolerances can add up to cause the collar to be eccentric to the cutter. The motor casting and spindle, the base casting fit to the motor, the subbase with respect to the screw hole pattern, the hole in the subbase, the slop of the collar in the cutter hole and the collet tolerance to the cutter. There is no way for a collar to be dead centered to the cutter. Plus or minus $\frac{1}{16}$″ of eccentricity is ordinary.

Another peculiarity specific to the collar is

that in every case the template collar is larger in outer diameter than the cutting circle diameter of the cutter. For straight-line work this means nothing, but for curvy template work it means the radii of the template have to be adjusted to the intended radius (Figure 4-17). Most top-bearing-guided cutters are the same diameter as the cutter, so this is not a problem.

A collar is in friction with its template so

Figure 4-16
This is the collection of collars I use. I have several duplicates. The same collar on two different routers with different cutters can simplify two-stage cuts. The same setup can be used because both cutters will cut on the same center.

there is some wear, although it is of little practical importance. Fortunately they have no moving parts and are virtually indestructible. The races (grooves) of a bearing, on the other hand, are subject to unbelievable accelerations and stresses and wear out frequently.

Typical Uses of Template Guides

I use the template guide to do most cross-grain work. I use a wide right-angle template (Figure 4-18) clamped to either the front or rear of the panel or board. This keeps the router off the work surface, which often has travel problems—squirming on surface tear-out and chips that won't escape under the subbase. A dado or dovetail way is a typical cross-grain operation. The template also makes setup easier since a direct measurement can be taken from its edge (Figure 4-19) and the work edge is always 90° to the edge of the workpiece. Three problems—the layout, the guide contrivance and the avoidance of chip interference—are all cared for with one simple tool, the template.

I use template guides for tenons, too (Figure 4-20). With the workpiece indexed on-end and the template adjusted, very precise two-faced tenons can be routed. I also do large or critical multistage cuts with the template-guide system first. In a lap, for instance, the excavations are so large they cannot be done in one-depth passes. Since the collar is always greater in diameter than the cutter, the net edges of the lap are not cut. The first stage of the laps I cut are 80 to 90 percent complete with the collar system. I cut the edge and the remainder of the depth with the shank-bearing cutter because of its accuracy. As a consequence I keep it sharper longer, because most of the cut was done with an unpiloted, cheaper and perhaps half-worn cutter whose cut may have been imperfect but otherwise cosmetically unimportant (Figures 4-21 and 4-22).

Nearly any template operation can be done or adjusted so that a collar system can be used. A pair of the 1¼″ O.D. (outside diameter) collars are great when using two routers with different or equal diameter cutters at different depths. Two cuts can be made with only one setup. A pair of 42039s (I.D. [inside diameter] = ¾″) are also quite useful for smaller cutters used in

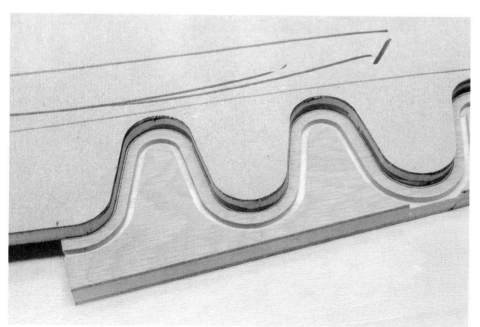

Figure 4-17
This "pathway" template cut is done with the guide constantly held against the template. Radii on the template don't match those on the workpiece. Inside radii are smaller and outside radii are copied larger.

Figure 4-18
This setup is very practical for cross-grain work. If you've had trouble working directly on the work face, you'll fare much better on the template.

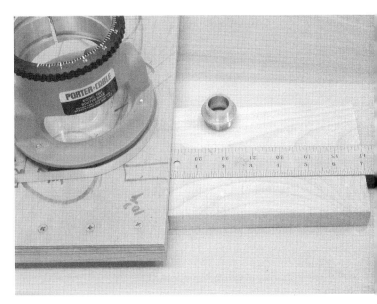

Figure 4-19
A direct measurement for the cross-grain setup is possible. Slide the template with its 90° reference member along the edge of stock. Now read directly from the template edge to the end of the board. Add one-half the diameter of the collar to the measurement to find the center line of the cut.

Figure 4-20
I can rout this relatively long two-faced tenon with a template, collar and straight bit. The workpiece is easily indexed on the end of the jig.

Figure 4-21
When I cut a lap, I first waste most of the cut with a collar guide and straight bit.

Figure 4-22

The second phase of the lap is done without disturbing the first setup. I just switch to another router that has a flush-cutting cutter installed and finish the cut right up to the template.

much the same way (see Porter Cable chart). The Porter Cable collar inventory has evolved over many years for many applications. As such their O.D.s, I.D.s and lengths are peculiar.

Ordinary shop templates are ⅛″ to ½″ thick. You will find that the collar lengths may not be compatible with your template thickness. If this should turn out to be the case, they can be shortened. The lengths are not critical, but they must be shorter than your template is thick. If you take the router base plate off and put it in a vise it can be used as a holder for the collar (Figure 4-23). A hacksaw can be used to cut it to length, then just clean up the face on the disk sander. You should deburr the new edge with steel wool or a file.

There are other, less popular ways of controlling the portable router. You can freehand the tool, for example, or use pantographs or other carriage systems. But most hand-routed operations use bearings, collars, bases or edge guides.

Figure 4-23

To shorten the collar, use the subbase and a clamp to hold the collar for a hacksaw cut. Use a ¼″-thick piece of plastic or plywood as a shield and as a guide for the hacksaw.

SPECIALTY TEMPLATE GUIDES BY PORTER CABLE

Purpose	Model no.	ID	OD	Distance Past Base
Stair routing 1 1/8" thick treads	42021	1 1/32"	1 1/4"	7/16"
Lock face routing	42024	21/32"	3/4"	9/16"
1/2" dovetailing & general routing	42027	11/32"	7/16"	5/32"
General routing	42030	25/32"	1"	3/8"
General routing	42033	13/32"	1/2"	5/16"
General routing	42036	9/32"	3/8"	5/16"
General routing	42039	3/4"	59/64"	9/16"
Hinge butt routing	42042	5/8"	51/64"	9/16"
For use with Stanley T-3 template	42045	17/32"	5/8"	9/16"
Omnijig template	42046	17/32"	5/8"	7/32"
For hinges with 5/8" corner radius	42048	1 3/8"	1 35/64"	17/32"
30mm Guide for 43936 bit	42050	27.94mm 1 7/64"	30mm 1 3/16"	10mm 25/64"
1/4" dovetailing	42054	1/4"	5/16"	5/32"
Stair routing 1 1/16" thick treads	45101	1 1/32"	1 1/4"	7/16"
Stair routing 1" thick treads	45102	1 3/64"	1 3/8"	7/16"
Lock nut for all template guides	42237			
Template Guide Kit contains template Nos. 42054, 42036, 42027, 42033, 42045, 42024, 42042 & Lock Nut 42237 (2)	42000			

CHAPTER FIVE
Using the Router Safely

Woodworking, in general, is hazardous. Almost every woodworking operation requires the removal of material with a sharp cutting tool. That fact alone should throw up a red flag of suspicion. I've heard some craftspeople go so far as to say: "There are only two kinds of woodworkers: those that *have* been injured and those that *will* be." Hazards and risks in routing are related not only to the router but also to the workpiece and the woodworker. The routing equipment is pretty safe stuff though, and just like with cars, most accidents are due to driver error—not to equipment factors. You gotta change your brake pads and bad tires, though, or all bets are off.

Every router's owner manual spells out some twenty or more safety rules that you'd better adhere to. I'll not repeat those here, but it would indeed be time well spent if you'd reread them after reading this chapter. In my view, the basis of safety and the reduction of risk is founded, first, on my body and its tolerance to injury (zilch) and, second, to the workpiece. Harm and irreversible mayhem can be inflicted on the workpiece, often at some risk to the operator; the two are closely and curiously interrelated.

Let's begin this journey with a checklist of responsibilities that you'll need to address to do an ordinary routing. Then let's look at the funda-

mentals of the setup and how they relate to safety. Finally I'll list the hazards specific to the routing equipment, and what you can do to save the workpiece and yourself from an accident. I would also like to take this opportunity to emphasize that there are many dangerous yet accepted woodworking procedures in the art, such as lowering a workpiece onto a spinning router bit or saw blade. This behavior makes me uncomfortable and, in spite of the acceptance of such procedures, I refuse to do them. I'll go so far as to redesign the workpiece so the operation is unnecessary before taking the risk. May I strongly advise you that no matter how well a procedure is accepted, if you feel uncomfortable about it, *don't do it.*

OPERATING CHECKLIST

There is an order to ready yourself and the router for a cutting. You can't, for instance, adjust the depth of cut before tightening the cutter in the collet. Let common sense be one of your guidelines, and think about what you're doing. The preparation for table routing is similar to that for hand routing, but there are special considerations for each. (The router table safety concerns are addressed in chapter ten.)

Securing the Workpiece

The workpiece and the cut are your first considerations. No matter how you've prepared the workpiece (jointed, planed and sawn for example), it has to be well secured. Ideally the workpiece and template (if required) each should be held fast in at least two places. Frequently two clamps, both on the same piece, are sufficient. Sometimes the workpiece is too small for two clamps, so it must be wedged and clamped. The template can be made oversized so the second clamp on it can be away from and not on the workpiece (Figure 5-1). Vacuum clamping is always acceptable, as is screwing the workpiece to another substrate. A router mat, a rubber friction surface, is accepted practice to hold small workpieces, but it's one of those practices I just don't feel comfortable with, so I don't use them. Spot glue and double-sided tape are also accepted hold-fast techniques, but not for me. Any adhesive regarded as temporary just doesn't ring out security in my view.

As a commonsense guideline, consider how much force you have to apply to the workpiece to rout it. Then apply twice that much (using the unplugged router) to the fixed workpiece. If it moves, it's not secured well enough. Be aggressive here, push down and sideways—if it moves you could ruin the cut or slip unexpectedly.

Securing the Cutter

Your next concern is securing the cutter. An unsecured or insufficiently tightened cutter is the source of a lot of grief. The cutter's shank must be smooth, free of any dings, and of correct and uniform diameter. You should measure the shank's diameter in two or three places to make

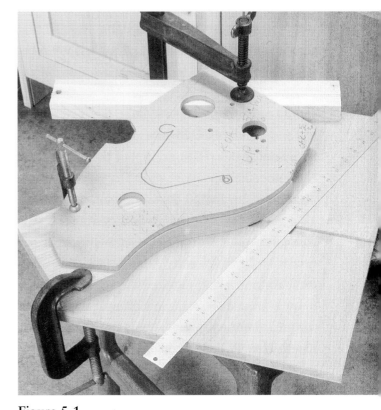

Figure 5-1

The template, as well as the workpiece, must be well secured. Making your templates larger than the workpiece, when you can, will make them easier to clamp.

small cutting diameters (say ⁵⁄₁₆″ or less) whose flutes are 1″ or longer are fragile and can break easily. Dovetail bits are also easy to break when there is significant grinding into the shank (Figure 5-10). Beware when using long skinny cutters to make deep cuts—they can break. A better strategy is to avoid their use. Any cutter that is marketed as fragile won't cut well anyway.

Figure 5-9
Both of these cutters are straight cutters and perform similar functions. The router bit, however, is a mere miniaturization of the 3-winged shaper cutter. The shaper cutter may cut ten times as much material before it needs to be sharpened, but it can't do any inside work.

The Trapped Cutter

Some router bits, as a result of their design, are trapped in the workpiece during the cut. If a cutter can be pulled aside (for edge cuts) or straight up (inside and some side cuts) without spoiling the cut, it is not trapped. A rabbet cutter along the edge can be pulled aside or up without a spoil, as can a straight bit, a roundover and a bevel. Dovetail, key way slotters or glue-joint bits are all stuck in the workpiece (Figure 5-11). If you rock or tilt the router or workpiece you'll spoil the cut, and in severe cases you may pull the cutter out of the collet. Some safe cutters, if used in an unorthodox fashion, can also be trapped (Figure 5-12). You must be aware of and avoid trapping the bit. With care and experience, not tipping the router for example, you can rout safely in spite of this entrapment problem. I point this out for your safety. Take small bites in small increments to gain confidence and skill. Woodworking is full of acceptable but hazardous practices. Knowledge and experience are your best defenses against a workpiece accident or an injury.

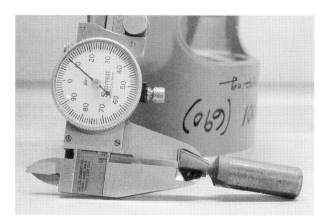

Figure 5-10
This quite ordinary 14° dovetail bit has just about an ⅛″ of material left in its shank after the grinding process. It will bend, flex and chatter the walls of the dovetail sockets it cuts.

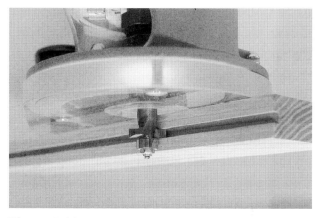

Figure 5-11
When using a slotter, or any cutter that is engaged inside the workpiece, you must keep the router flat at all times. If you rock the router you will spoil the cut, and you may pull the cutter from the collet.

Figure 5-12

I would never rout with the tool bit trapped under the workpiece like this. The risk is there for a kick-back, a burn or tear-out, and the loss of control of the router.

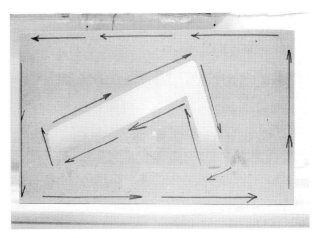

Figure 5-13

Follow the arrows on this template for the safest and most efficient direction of cutting on inside or outside cuts.

STARTING THE CUT— THE ANTI-CLIMB WAY

Safe hand routing is done counterclockwise around the outside of the work and clockwise on through or blind inside work (Figure 5-13). This counterclockwise feed direction is prescribed for your safety. Since the cutter cuts in clockwise rotation, a feed direction that is counterclockwise is against the cutter rotation. In this mode of operation there is little danger of kickback. The cutting is done most efficiently, but at the risk of tear-out. Very sharp cutters, an appropriate feed rate, good wood and other factors can minimize the tear-out, but it is a threat nonetheless. However, I must emphasize that it is the safest way to hand rout.

THE CLIMB CUT

If you feed the router clockwise around the outside of the stock and counterclockwise on the inside (exactly opposite to the anti-climb cut), there is some risk. There is more risk when taking heavy cuts. This clockwise feed is known as climb cutting. If you were to replace the cutter with a small rubber tire and feed the router clockwise, it would probably fly right out of your hands—and herein lies the danger, namely the possible loss of control of the tool. The risk is real and, for the novice, making this mistake may discourage you from routing ever again. For that reason and for the sake of familiarity, I strongly advise that you do not climb cut until you have several hundred hours of successful anti-climb routing experience behind you.

If you can execute acceptable, safe and consistent cuts with the handheld router you may want to try the climb cut. Why? Because the climb cut produces almost no tear-out! However, it also is not as efficient, so more horsepower and hand forces are required than for the same cut done anti-climb. If you decide to learn the climb cut, begin with very light cuts, $^{3}/_{16}''$ square or less. Always consider climb cutting as a risk.

At this stage you're ready to rout. Do your level best to get comfortable, keep from snagging the cord set, and work in a well-lit area.

Figure 6-7

Here I've band sawn the luan and routed the oak with the bevel cutter. When you rout a lot of material, saw away the waste before committing your router.

Figure 6-8

If you have a lot of mortises or other inside work to do, map out the area and drill away most of the waste. You'll save your cutters unnecessary wear and tear and you'll get done sooner.

Figure 6-9

With this 3-wing carbide drill you can drill near-perfect holes in many different kinds of materials. If you saw away some of the circle you can use it as a template. This drill is 2½" in diameter!

LAYOUT AND MEASURING

I used to measure and scribe everything. As I made more and more stuff, though, it occurred to me that such precision and attention to detail was largely unnecessary! I am a furniture maker and the things I make stand up by themselves and don't necessarily have to fit in tight quarters. For those of you fitting in built-in and kitchen cabinets, most of your measurements may be critical. For me it's more important that like pieces are the same size. An ⅛" here or a ¼" there in the overall dimension of a piece is of little consequence to me. A tape measure is all I need for the bulk of structural elements in a piece of furniture. I do, however, have to take great pains ensuring that my setups, fences and stops do not budge when I'm gang cutting the parts (Figure 6-10).

Close measurement comes into play when I'm into the joinery and the fitting of the accessories. The accessories I'm talking about here include such things as guides and slides, door pulls, panels, drawers and shelving. These all re-

Figure 6-10

Once I've set up the coordinates for the mortise on my mortiser I use a stop to locate the workpiece. Each subsequent workpiece is butted against the stop and held with at least two toggle clamps.

Figure 6-11
Take a lot of careful measurements to fit a door flush and inset. Close tolerances pay off.

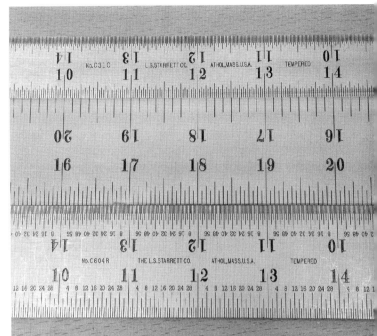

Figure 6-12
Starrett probably has the best assortment of scales and rules. These are nicely ruled to ¹⁄₆₄″.

quire close measuring and endless calculations to ensure a good fit. The sizing of a mortise and tenon door with a tongued panel that fits into an opening (flush inset design), for example (Figure 6-11), requires a dozen or so very accurate measurements. The length and width of the opening, the length of the stiles and rails, the depths of mortises and their lengths and widths, the tenons, the panel glue up and subsequent dimensioning of its tongues and the geometry of the slots to receive it, the location of the pull and its centers for the holes for the hardware and the hinges all have to be accurately accounted for.

Scales And Rules

I use quality tools for measuring. Precision scales of 1, 2 and 3 feet graduated in ¹⁄₈″, ¹⁄₁₆″, ¹⁄₃₂″ and ¹⁄₆₄″ are necessities for me (Figure 6-12). I have to read ¹⁄₆₄″ with a magnifier—but I don't have to do it too often. A center rule, a rule with a zero in the center (Figure 6-13), is a real time saver when you're working with centerlines.

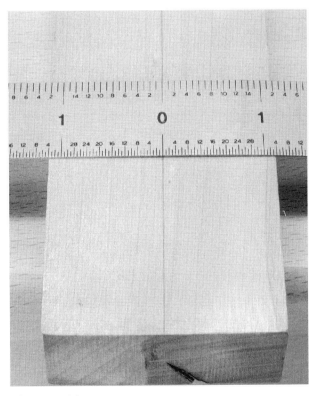

Figure 6-13
This rule, with its center (zero) on the midline of the rule, is just great to find the center of a workpiece. You can also use it to lay out points equidistant from the centerline of your stock.

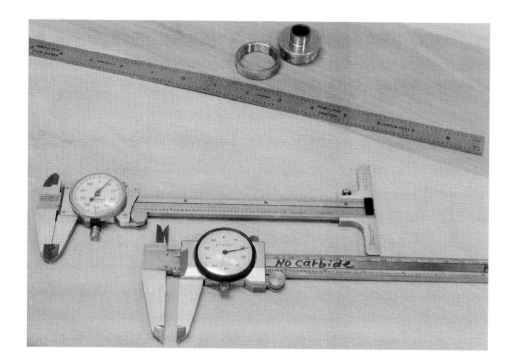

Figure 6-14
Mitutoyo and Starrett dial calipers. These tools can measure depth and inside and outside dimensions. The depth accessory is fastened to the Starrett tool.

Bridge City Tool, Starrett, Brown and Sharp and Mitutoyo are names associated with quality measurement and setup tools. The various-length scales are needed not only for outside length measurements, but also for easy and precise inside measurements.

Dial Caliper

I use a dial caliper for careful thickness measurements. I strongly recommend a machinist's caliper from one of the companies mentioned (Figure 6-14), not one of the plastic look-alikes so often found in woodworking catalogs. These tools are either metric or English, and measure depth and inside and outside dimensions (e.g., bearings and mortises). The dial caliper usually measures to the nearest .001″, which is as close as you'll ever have to measure in woodworking. It is also invaluable in keeping track of your tool bits. You can measure all of their diameters and determine just how much carbide your sharpening service is taking to true up your cutters. I

recommend a tool with a 6″ capacity. Dial calipers are precision tools—if you drop one you'll probably ruin it, so keep it in its case and treat it with care.

Squares and Straightedges

Just as important as calipers are ground straightedges and machinist's squares. A 45° and a 90° fixed machinist's square (Figures 6-15 and 6-16) are essential for accurate machine and jig setup, calibration and layout. Jigs and fixtures that you expect precision and accuracy from must be precision made. The critical indexing and workpiece resting positions of your jigs and fixtures should all be referenced from precision-ground tools to avoid handicapping your entire woodworking experience (Figures 6-17 and 6-18).

The Ground Straightedge

There are many examples of straightedges that are acceptable for general work. Some scales are shear cut and others might be stamped. If, how-

Figure 6-15
Bridge City makes excellent layout, checking and setup tools. This miter square, for example, is being used to verify this flat miter.

Figure 6-16
This Starrett square with its nice long beam is used here in calibrating my right-angle template.

ever, you want to really find out just how straight and flat your jointer tables or saw surfaces and fences are and if you can actually straighten and true a board, you'll need a ground straightedge. If you are satisfied with average work, and tracking errors is something you don't want to involve yourself with, then an ordinary 1′ or 2′ scale (a rafter square, for example) will do you just fine.

On the other hand, if the pursuit of control and excellence is your goal then a precision-ground straightedge is necessary. If your fence

has a "hollow" in it or is warped, you can see it with the ground straightedge. If your jointer tables twist or sag you can true them with shims and gibs only if you have a ground straightedge. The jointer is your trueing tool. If it lies to you, every subsequent operation (sawing, planing, drilling, joining, sanding or whatever) is suspect. Your straightedge is also invaluable in the construction and calibration of jigs and fixtures (Figure 6-19). If you spring for a 4′ edge you'll have a lot of tool. You'll easily verify most saw tables and jointers with it, as well as the straightness of

Figure 6-17
The fence on my tenon-making end worker has to be 90° to the work surface.

Figure 6-18
I use my sander to sand the ends of stock square. Its fence has to be 90° to the platen, as shown here.

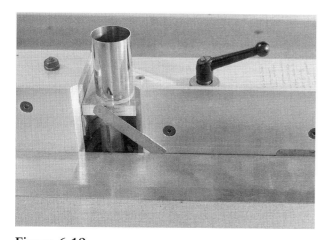

Figure 6-19
The fences on my jointer have to be parallel to produce straight edges. Here I'm using a .020" feeler gauge and the straightedge to adjust the fences.

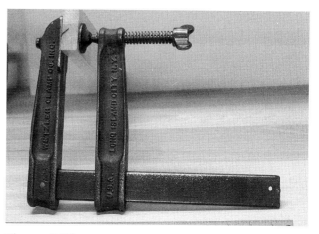

Figure 6-20
This Wetzler quick acting clamp has a 7" reach and you can squeeze maybe 500 lbs. with it. Most clamps require two hands to operate, as this one does.

freshly jointed edges and surfaces. A shorter one, 1' to 2', is a lot handier for calibrating most jigs.

CLAMPING TOOLS

Routing is an exercise in clamping. One of the main advantages of stationary routing is the absence of clamping; the workpiece is simply slid past the cutter. Nevertheless, the router table itself often will require you to clamp down safety devices, fences and stops. Portable routing is all clamping. The workpiece, templates, stops, jigs, etc. all have to be clamped, and to be safe each element needs *two* clamps. There are a lot of choices, but in my view there are only three types of clamping tools useful for routing.

The Quick Acting Slide Clamp
I prefer Wetzlers' quick acting slide jamming clamps over all the others. A jaw depth of 5", 7" and 9" will cover most of your routing demands.

Rarely are the combined thicknesses of bench, workpiece and template greater than 8", so the jaw opening needn't be a lot greater (Figure 6-20). A lot of reach is important in hand routing because a router needs a clear pathway for a safe trip. If the clamps are too close to the work edge you have to clamp and unclamp to rout. Most router bases are under 7" in diameter, so if you can keep 4" between the work edge and the clamp swivel pad you should be in for a clear sail. The quick action is important for speed of setup, and this design is particularly resistant to loosening under vibration.

The C-Clamp
For those instances where the clamp force is quite distant from the router work site, an ordinary C-clamp is preferred. Any clamp with an opening from 4" to 10" and a throat of at least 2½" will do. C-clamps are also good at maintaining squeeze with vibration, and they press much harder than a fast acting clamp (Figure 6-21).

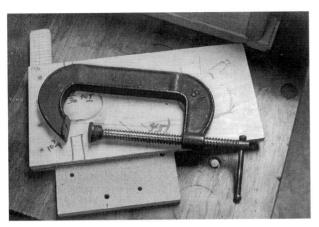

Figure 6-21

This Jorgensen C-clamp is capable of loads to 1,500 lbs. The C-clamp also requires two hands to operate. They are nice for clamping templates, stops and fences that might be under intense vibration.

The Toggle Clamp

The third type of clamp I like is the toggle clamp. When the same clamping forces are repeatedly necessary, as in a routine or production application, toggle clamps are indispensable. There is a design for most applications, and they are cheap and very resistant to loosening (Figure 6-22). One to five-hundred pound forces are easily achieved with toggle clamps, but be advised that at these loads they can bend and distort your fixture. These separating forces do not exist with C-clamps. There are many plunger designs, and some styles even compensate for different thicknesses of workpieces (Figure 6-23).

Bar, band, spring and hand screw clamps are important to have around the shop but are of little value (save spring clamps for temporary hold down) for routing applications.

Routing is peculiar. If you were to chain saw or band saw most of your projects, rough, even green, wood would probably be acceptable to you. You'd never know just how demanding the tooling is for routing. Most of us start out with somebody else's processed wood and get by with the table or radial saw, some hand tools and

Figure 6-22

This toggle clamp has been modified for edge-guide clearance on my mortiser. The tool can be activated with one hand and quite quickly. It is rated at 500 lbs. Be aware that a jig can bend and contort at such pressures with toggle clamps.

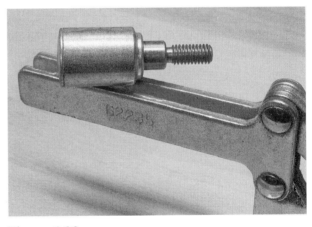

Figure 6-23

This plunger is internally spring loaded and can compensate for minor thickness variations in the workpiece.

maybe a drill press. This approach isolates us from the technology as well. It is when you're into routing and shaper work that all these restrictions and demands on dimensioning, layout and setup become apparent. Routing, as a primary woodworking process, is quite tool-room dependent. It's the nature of the process.

CHAPTER SEVEN

The Router Setting

Aworkshop where the router is the primary tool is best set up where there is a central bench for it. In my shop the stationaries are essentially lined along the walls. The router stuff is in the middle. I use a bench accessible from all sides and a beam fixture that I often fasten to the top of the router table. The router table is pulled into the center of the shop when needed as well. As an instructor of routing, I'm often presenting myself and my gear in a distant classroom or shop, and what I've learned from that experience has been transposed into the shop furniture I use.

ESTABLISH A COMFORTABLE HEIGHT

Routing, whether portable or stationary, is unlike most other woodworking processes. Many router cuttings can and have been produced with the table saw, jointer and hand tools. When you pass a workpiece through the saw blade or along the jointer fence, the process is relatively comfortable and effective. Plowing, molding, hammer-chisel work, planing and other hand-tool operations are also relatively comfortable. In the one case your back, arms and legs are at work pushing wood. This is also true for the

hand operations, though chisel work is relatively close-quartered compared to, say, ripping an 8' board. Hundreds of years of tradition have led the way to established work surface heights for these operations. Sawing, jointing and shaping (stationary tool work) are usually done on a work surface 32″ to 34½″ from the floor; bench work (hand-tool woodworking) is a little higher, maybe 34″ to 36½″.

Electric routing, although a nearly 90-year-old practice, is usually treated as a hand-tool process and is therefore performed at standard bench-work heights. Routing is rather complex in that it requires careful hand/eye coordination, a proper feed rate, judicious setup and strength. Handling a router is like handling no other tool. Most hand tools, and indeed a lot of electric tools, are well under 3 to 4 lbs.; a router is 8 to 15 lbs. Repetitive or occasional router hand work is tiring and difficult to do well at a 34″ to 36″ bench height. The router bit is difficult to see and your neck and shoulders quickly fatigue in a crouched posture. The struggle to monitor the cutting and stay within the confines of your jigging is simply not practical at 34″ to 36″.

The best height to rout is different for everybody. Although we can all be seated in the same size chair in an auditorium, some of us will be more comfortable than others: 39″ to 41″ is the

Figure 7-1
I designed this 40"-high beam so I can work comfortably and more safely than bending over the typical 35" bench.

Figure 7-2
Design plenty of overhang into your workbench. Routing is clamping, and the top overhang here makes clamping very easy.

ideal router working height for me, I'm 73" tall (Figure 7-1). You can experiment with heights by hand routing on the drill press table.

The drill press table can usually be adjusted from 0" to 45" plus from the floor. Clamp some stock on the table, do some practice cuts, adjust the table height and cut some more. You'll know when you've found the correct height because you'll be able to see the cutter and the work without stooping. Your neck and shoulders won't tire and your arms will rest comfortably on the router grips or offset subbase knob.

Workbench Design Considerations

Insufficient bench top overhang and the location of the bench in most shops are usually such that the routing process is encumbered. Moreover, most benches are appointed with tool trays, vises, cabinets, drawers and such, so that clamping is difficult if not impossible. A routing workbench, to be of any use, has to have plenty of free overhang and access to any side (Figure 7-2).

Routing is clamping. Setting up opposite-handed parts (e.g., the left and right sides of a

Figure 7-4

I had the fixed end of this No. 175 Jorgensen C-clamp welded to a predrilled ¼″-thick piece of steel. I screwed the clamp to the underside of the beam so it only takes one hand to operate it and it's always handy.

the straightest boards for the best resistance to distortion. Mill the board or boards to 1″ plus or minus ¹⁄₁₆″. This simple but unbraced structure is rigid at 1″—it may not be at a lesser thickness. The knock-down joinery is simply shallow tongues and grooves reinforced with steel cross dowels and bolts (Figure 7-5). I chose knock-down assembly for strength, and I can always take it apart for repairs. Moreover, if I need to add on a fixture or jig I can work the individual elements rather than contending with the whole assembly.

I designed my jig with an 8″ overhang to facilitate clamping (Figure 7-6). The other 2 feet of the underside of the beam is essentially clear of all clamp obstacles so a workpiece can be clamped virtually anywhere on either side of the jig. The work surface also has a through keyhole slot (Figure 7-7) in it so a router, even with its cutter extended, can rest flat (subbase down) over the hole. The keyhole is simply decorative camouflage used to hide an accident I had when I accidentally started a router in the hole. A 1½″ hole is all that is necessary.

I put a stick on the edge of the end piece,

Figure 7-5

I routed some shallow tongues and grooves to register the component parts of the beam. Then I drilled through the joints for joint connector bolts as shown here. The beam is not glued together so I can always take it apart to repair it or add stuff on.

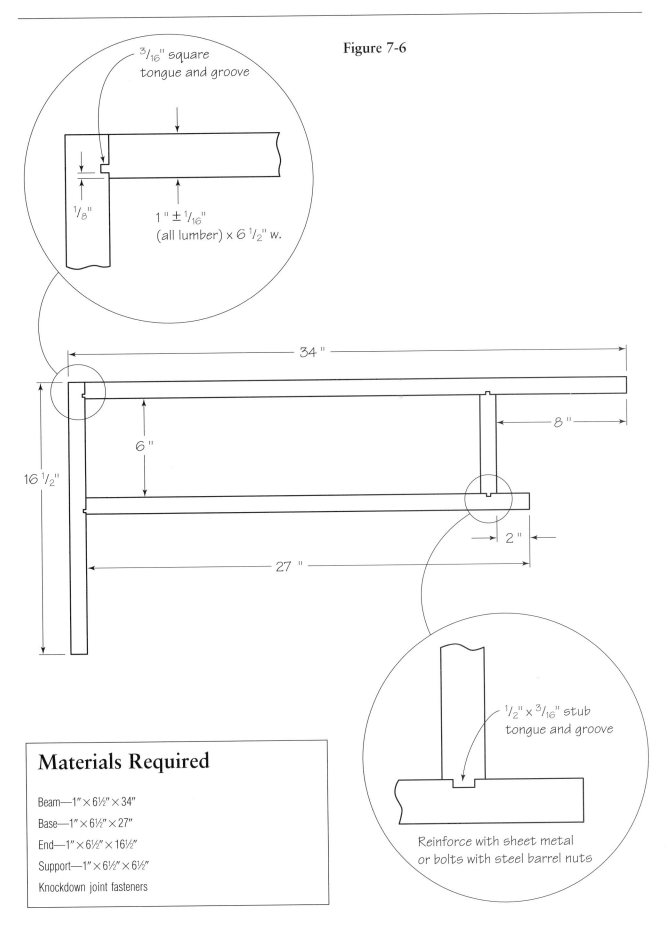

Figure 7-6

$^3/_{16}$" square
tongue and groove

$^1/_8$"

1 " ± $^1/_{16}$"
(all lumber) × 6 $^1/_2$" w.

34 "

8 "

6 "

16 $^1/_2$"

27 "

2 "

$^1/_2$" × $^3/_{16}$" stub
tongue and groove

Reinforce with sheet metal
or bolts with steel barrel nuts

Materials Required

Beam—1" × 6½" × 34"

Base—1" × 6½" × 27"

End—1" × 6½" × 16½"

Support—1" × 6½" × 6½"

Knockdown joint fasteners

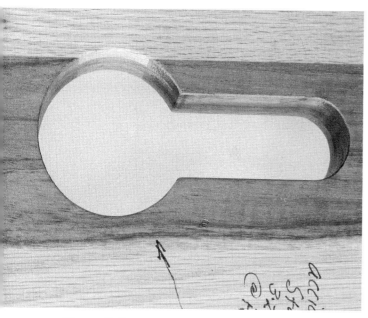

Figure 7-7

I routed this keyhole slot to waste away a splintered-up mess I made when I accidentally started a router. A 1½" or 2" hole in the beam will allow you to rest your router with an extended cutter flat on its subbase.

Figure 7-8

I bolted this maple fence to the edge of the end piece. It serves to register any workpiece, like the one shown here, square to the top of the jig.

which is flush to the inside and situated 1¾" below the work surface (Figure 7-8). The stick measures 1″ × 1¾″ × 17″ and is square to the work surface (Figure 7-9). It functions as a stop and as a reference for stock indexed vertically. Using a 90° template, template collars and assorted bits I can make sliding dovetails, two faced tenons, slots or decorative end cuts on stock to 6½" wide (Figures 7-10, 7-11, and 7-12). If end cuts are important to you, make the width of the jig consistent with the width of the boards you intend to rout. If you'd like, you can omit any joinery and just use cleats and Number 12 or 14 flathead sheet metal screws to screw it together. If

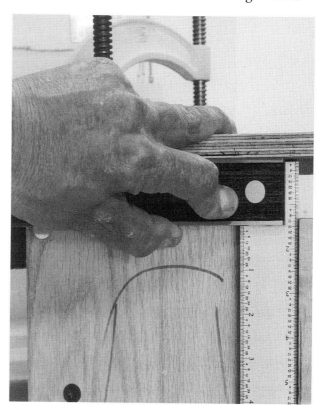

Figure 7-9

Check the fence-to-surface squareness as shown. If you cut the end panel square and if the beam that goes into it is 90° to the outside face of the panel, then the fence will be square to the work surface. If it isn't, try to shim it square or just mount the fence on the face rather than the edge. It's easier to square up if it's mounted on the face.

you screw into end grain, use at least 3″-long screws.

Woodworking with a 10-lb. electric hand router is indeed different than working with most other woodshop tools. The comfortable working height, lighting and work surface considerations are unique. The router beam will help some, or perhaps a new top on an old workbench with lots of overhang will be your choice. On-site work is easy too. Simply take your router table to the job and use the beam on it for those cuttings you can't do on the router table. I've hauled the beam, the router table and a Milwaukee vacuum all in a Honda Civic.

Figure 7-11
The second cut on this tenon produces a two-faced centered tenon. Your workpiece has to be well dimensioned for a reversal cut because each of its edges is referenced separately off the fence.

Figure 7-10
You can take big bites off a workpiece on-end like this. Nevertheless, get some practice taking ³⁄₈″- to ⁵⁄₈″-long cuts before trying a big dovetail.

Figure 7-12
Experiment—sooner or later you can use what you've learned in a folly. Here I'm using a subbase guide to control the lateral depth of cut on a series of stripes cut at different but even steps.

CHAPTER EIGHT
Router Bits

The router bit puts you in contact with the work. Everything you've done to this point in preparation for the routing is now ready to be expressed. Your judgment on the depth of cut, your choice of router, selection of cutter, method of securing the work and the type of work you've planned are about to be tested. If your preparation is reasonable and if you've matched the horsepower to the depth of cut and feed rate you will get a good result. The more you rout the better your results will be, and that is the key to good router woodworking. If you take a new or troublesome routing procedure and practice it enough you will be good at it. You will make mistakes, and I hope you do (on scrap, that is), but this is the pathway to success. It is possible that you are very talented and that you always get it right the first time. But for the majority of us, excellence is preceded by hard work.

I'm not trying to discourage you from a life of woodworking. I am, however, suggesting that if you'd like professional results you should practice to a level that is consistent with your ability. It takes just as much time and energy to do a crummy job as it does to do a good job, so why not do at least acceptable work?

You might now ask what does all this have to do with router bits? Well, not much—except that the quality of your routings is far more dependent on you than on the cutter and the router. Just as unexpectedly, I strongly suspect that if you did the same cut with ten new cutters from ten manufacturers you couldn't tell the difference. Furthermore, if the cut was done with ten different cutters freshly resharpened by a reputable sharpening service, you couldn't tell the difference either.

CHOOSING A BIT

The router bit business is fiercely competitive, and most brand-name tools perform similarly and admirably. Router bits, nonetheless, are somewhat different; some are better than others, but not that much better. In my twenty-plus years as a routing woodworker I've tried a lot of router bits and so I'm in a good position to notice excellence or mediocrity in a new or reground cutter. For the most part, the old names in cutter manufacturing are old because their product is acceptable. You would be well advised to buy Porter Cable, Bosch, Wisconsin Knife, Paso Robles Carbide, Eagle or Amana. However, if you must have the best, the new guy in town, CMT, is the standard to which I now compare the competition. CMT cutters are very well balanced and brightly painted orange for visibility and corrosion resistance. Their cutters are of anti-kickback design, nicely finished, always well ground and sharp, and they last longer than most cutters. Consider CMT as the industry standard—the competition does.

Examine Bit Features

There are dozens of features of router bits, some known only to the manufacturer, that can be graded and compared. However, for most of us router bits from as many sources will last about as long and cut just about the same.

Cutters can be categorized in terms of size, materials, whether they join, mill or decorate, or whether they will accept bearings (Figure 8-1). There are other subcategories such as laminate trim or cutting, solid surface (Corian et al.), door/drawer, architectural and so on. There are probably 1,500 different cutters from perhaps 30 or 40 suppliers or manufacturers in North America. The subject has been covered by every

woodworking magazine and dozens of books related to woodcraft. I advise you to get the cutter catalogs from those companies just mentioned and others that I have listed in the sources of supply. The catalogs will educate you on cutter materials and design and describe their inventory in detail. They may also enlighten you as to what the future may bring in new cutters or manufacturing breakthroughs.

In my view the information is both valid and interesting, and will assist you in selecting the right tool, but for basic knowledge and an understanding of the differences, there is simply no substitute for hands-on practice. There are, however, some general principles you should know about that are not, shall we say, "highlighted in the literature." Allow me to elaborate.

One or More Flutes

The number of cutting edges of a given cutter is certainly related to the quality of the finish. One of the main reasons for multiple flutes is tool balance, not finish. Small single-flute tools whose

Figure 8-1
In this assortment of cutters are typical examples of (from left to right) steel only, carbide-faced, solid carbide, shank-bearing guided and end-bearing guided cutters.

Figure 8-2
I cut each rabbet with a ½" straight bit. One of the cuts was done with a single flute; the other was cut with two flutes. Which is which?

cutting diameters are about equal to their shank diameters cut about as well as the same-size tool with two or more flutes. In a production situation where RPM, power and feed rates are carefully controlled, differences can be seen and measured between single and multiflute bits. But in general shop use, I can produce cuttings from 1-, 2- or 3-fluted bits that are indistinguishable from one another (Figure 8-2). Very high speed strobe photography has revealed that in the case of multifluted bits one flute usually does all or most of the cutting. Photomicrographs will often show more nicks on one flute than another, and that one flute is significantly sharper than the other after prolonged use. Imagine how much more service we would get between sharpenings if both flutes cut equally well. Nevertheless, multifluted bits are necessary for balance; moreover, only small diameter straight bits can be single fluted.

Cutter Life

The life of a cutter is dependent on the cutter, its materials and the material being routed, none of which you can do much about. The life is also related to the feed rate, stock removal, direction of cut (cross grain, down grain, climb cut, etc.) and the power of the router—and this you can do something about. That is to say you do play more than a casual role in determining the life of the cutters you use. Just how do you know when you're getting the best from your cutters? Well, I don't know how to describe this to you exactly, to you but I can tell you, you'll know when you're doing it right when the following conditions occur.

No Kickback

If and when you're routing and the workpiece or the router jumps back, it can often be your fault. There are many reasons for kickback, and bad stock is one of them. Often a workpiece can change shape due to stress relief during a cut, or the stick can be bent to begin with. I think the next most common cause is a mismatch of feed rate, power and depth of cut. Simply put, the operator is taking too much wood. Consistent with overbite is cutter wear.

If you're taking too much wood, the cutter heats up because you have to feed slower; a hot cutter means friction, which transmutes a sharp cutter into a dull cutter. Another way of saying this is, if there is no tendency to kickback and you're not burning wood, you're doing something right.

No Burning

Burning wood is due solely to friction. Router bits slice and fling wood away; they're not designed to burn it. A dull cutter doesn't cut very efficiently at any feed rate or depth of cut, and simply burns wood from too much abrasion. You can burn wood with a new cutter, too, if your feed rate is too slow. This often happens when routing all four sides of a workpiece because making the turn from long (down) grain to end grain is done too slowly (Figure 8-3). The trip around the corners is precarious because only one-fourth of the router is on the workpiece. An offset subbase will alleviate this problem. Notwithstanding, the moment burning occurs the cutter sharpness deteriorates rapidly. Burning wood can wear down carbide faster than aggressive but appropriate use. So if you're scorching wood, you're doing it wrong—and the cutter life will be at a minimum.

No Tear-Out

Tear-out, like kickback, is frequently caused by crummy wood. Interlocking grain, rowed grain, grain changes, stress and poorly dimensioned stock all contribute to tear-out (Figure 8-4). Sharp cutters, shallow cuts and well-matched feed rates can minimize tear-out, the latter all being in your control. If you always or frequently tear-out you're doing it wrong. Tear-out is consistent with high cutter wear because sharp cutters don't tear-out as much as dull ones. We are talking about cutter life here, and indirectly

Figure 8-3
The cutter used on this piece is still sharp enough to cut long grain without burning, but notice how it burns the end grain. Cross-grain and end-grain cuts are equally abusive to the cutting edges of router bits.

Figure 8-4
Tear-out like this is akin to a flat tire on a bicycle. Both phenomena are natural outcomes of their endeavors but they can be minimized.

about the quality of the routing. Adjusting the feed rate and depths of cut to match the work will cut way down on tear-out and increase cutter life.

Figure 8-5
The ¼″-thick 3-wing slotter produces the same cut as the ¼″ straight bit, only it's a lot quieter. The slotter acts like a saw blade, has lots of clearance, and flings the chip right out of the slot. The straight bit slams into both sides of its slot and the chip is trapped and recut.

No Noise

A certain amount of noise beyond idle is expected. Clearly the high-speed cutting action of a router bit engaged in combat is noisy. However, if the cutter is sharp and you've matched the power and feed rate to the profile (the cutter shape) being cut, there isn't a lot more noise above idle.

Noise is indeed a strange form of energy that can't be measured by your ear. What I am asking here is for you to tune into a characteristic noise level that is consistent with efficiency. If you want to know exactly what I'm talking about, get a new CMT ⅜″ rabbet bit. Set the depth for about ¼″ and rout along the edge of a piece of hardwood with a low-mileage router having 1½ horsepower or more. This anti-kick-back cutter is so well balanced and sharp you can rout just about as slow or fast as you'd like and the results are going to be good. Pay particular attention to the noise: the intensity, the racket from the motor and the cutting noise. It is the benchmark for noise that you should strive for in any routing task. In my view, most routings can be done at about the same noise level. It

might take a big router, a small bite, a two-stage cut, a different cutter (a rabbetter vs. a straight bit or a slotter, for instance), a pre-machine operation—whatever—but most router cuttings can be done rather quietly (Figure 8-5). When the din and blast is like the condition I described in chapter five, you're doing it wrong. Excessive noise is a guarantee of excessive cutter wear.

The Cutter Profile

Router bits bend, deflect and squirm under power. The longer the flute and the smaller the diameter, the more the flex: ¼″ bits bend a lot more than ½″ cutters. A cutter that is cutting a pathway is climb cutting on one side of the path and anti-climb cutting on the other. The bottom of the pathway is also being cut, so the tool is not only bending from side to side, it is being deflected opposite to its direction of travel. If a cutter has been subjected to excessive grinding into its shank, such as with dovetail cutters, the bending is only further aggravated.

Edge cuts are quite tolerant to flex. In fact, a cutter that badly chatters on both sides of its pathway on an inside cut can often cut perfectly along the edge of stock, though it may require some extra skill to do so (Figure 8-6). When an edge cut is labored or when an inside cut is chattered due to overfeed or a weak-kneed cutter, the friction increases and the cutter quickly dulls. Moreover the profile on the stock will be larger than the cutter. This increase in profile can be measured and may exceed $\frac{1}{32}''$ or more. If the profiles you cut are not equal to the cutter, you're doing it wrong. You may be doing the best you can with a weak or fragile cutter, but if the profile doesn't closely match the geometry of the cutter, the cutter will wear out quickly.

As a rule, decorative cutters are either large and inflexible or dainty and used only in shallow applications (veining and fluting, for example). Decorative cuts therefore are not suspect here; you may have to do more sanding than you'd like if the cutter deflects, but no harm is done. It is in the arena of joinery that cutter flex is problematic. Joinery is quite challenging, whether hand cut or machine cut. Add to that the inability to predict the width of a routed dovetail, slot or a mortise and you've got double trouble.

Cutter Mileage

A router bit is indeed special; A whole industry is dependent on it. In the production environment, large cutters with $\frac{3}{4}''$ or $1''$ shanks are typical and the machinery is much more sophisticated than the hand tools most of us are familiar with. With special materials, diamond matrix for instance, well-controlled depths of cut and power feeders, cutter lengths-of-run may measure in the thousands of feet. A well-made carbide straight bit with a $\frac{1}{2}''$ shank in the small shop or in the hands of a hobbyist may last only a few hundred feet. That is not a lot of cutting (ten trips around a 4×8 sheet of plywood or perhaps a hundred $4''$-long mortises) in terms of footage, and it is even more painful when you think of it in terms of time. A typical hand-fed feed rate might be $15'$ to $20'$ a minute. At that rate you'd be lucky to get more than one hour of use from even the best of cutters. An hour's worth of cutting at 20,000 cuts per minute is over a million cuts, and that's a lot more cuts than you'd ever get from a hand tool. Pay attention to the depth of cut, feed rate, noise, tearout, kickback pressure, burning and chatter. Share the cuttings with the stationaries when

Figure 8-6

This narrow dovetail cutter has a nick in its body, further weakening it. In spite of its fragility it cuts quite well on long-grain outside cuts.

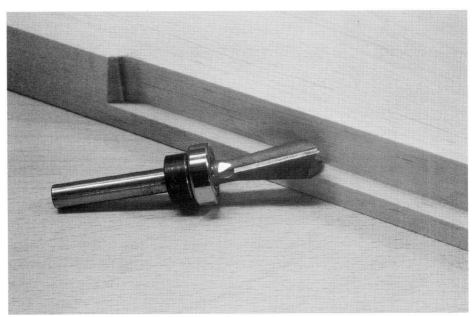

Figure 8-7A

I dinged this cutter with a wrench; it still cuts, but it leaves an unacceptable and noticeable line on the work. In a two-stage cut where the second stage is cut with another router and cutter, this profile would be acceptable because it will be erased by the cutter following it.

Figure 8-7B

Another strategy to extend the life of a cutter is to use it in a router table. The bottom of this bevel cutter (near the bearing) is worn out. The top half of the cutter (now extended into the playing field) has never seen wood and cuts like new. Adjusting the fence so the unused section of the cutter gets some use evens out the wear on the cutter.

you can and take heavy cuts in stages. I often cut the first stage with a half-worn or "cosmetically compromised" cutter and save the final pass for the newer tool with the better edge (Figure 8-7). Develop strategies to prolong precious cutter life.

Shank Size

The shank size is important to the cut quality and is indirectly related to the cutter life. Typical U.S. shank diameters are ¼″, ⁵⁄₁₆″, ⅜″ and ½″. Most cutter designs can be rendered on ½″ shanks. The ¼″ and ⅜″ shanks are great for small cutters and shallow bites, and light-duty routers often accept only them. If, however, you do a lot of routing, a ½″ tool is essential. Incidentally, you'll find that larger shanks are usually a better value, and they last longer too. Tool-bit deflection is your enemy and ½″ shanks are overwhelmingly stiffer than ¼″ bits.

The length of shank is important too. A long shank, at least 1¼″, is more apt to accept a shank bearing, and for safety at least ¾″ of the shank should be in the collet. If given a choice between two suppliers with the same cutter geometry, I'll usually select the longer shanked tool (Figure 8-8).

Plunging Bits

Most bits without bottom bearings are ground to cut on the end of the flute. However, only a few cutters are ground so you can plunge them straight into a workpiece like a drill. Most of the bottom-cutting bits have to be swept as they plunge or they won't cut on the bottom (Figure 8-9). This is both a nuisance and somewhat of a risk. For side cuts or interior cuts approached through the side this is no problem, but for a blind inside cut like a mortise it can be.

Figure 8-9

The pattern left in the workpiece illustrates just where this cutter is bottom cutting. This tool must be swept into the workpiece to bottom cut. Plunge cutting straight into a workpiece without a plunging cutter can be dangerous since the cutter will self-feed.

Figure 8-8

Router bits shouldn't be too long since they are supported (in the collet) such a long way from the cutter end. Nevertheless, long-shanked cutters work surprisingly well. Even these specialized cutters work well beyond my expectations. For safety's sake 2" of shank and cutter beyond the end of the collet is all I like to contend with.

Mortising is tedious work. The setup is time-consuming and to do good work your jigging has to be pretty good. Mortises are small and confined compared to most routings, and the ability to plunge straight down anywhere within the confines of the mortise is a safety plus. A cutter that won't plunge cut (with the router held still) can cause you to lose control, because the cutter will drive the router or self feed as it searches for its maximum depth. Furthermore, the inability to plunge straight down like a drill press takes more skill, since plunging, sweeping and adjusting cutter height under power take a lot of attention. (Remember: Plunge routing is done well only with a plunge router.)

Fortunately there are plunge-ground cutters just for this work, but it would be a nice safety benefit if all bottom-cutting bits could plunge

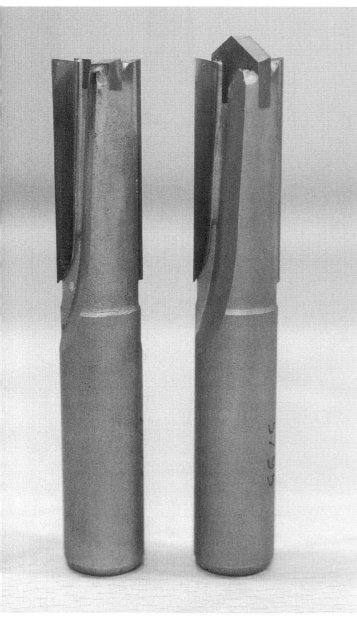

plunge cut. Some high-speed steel bits can also be ground for straight plunging. If you plan on a lot of blind cuts, and mortising in particular, ask your supplier for plunge-cutting bits that actually cut as you plunge straight, 90°, into a workpiece (Figure 8-10).

Carbide Or Steel Bits?

This is about like asking your consumer electronics people whether stereo is preferred over monophonic sound. Solid carbide or carbide-faced high-speed steel (HSS) is the standard in the woodworking industry today. High-speed steel bits are still around, but they wear out fast. For occasional use and if you get a kick out of sharpening, high-speed steel is acceptable. Furthermore, HSS bits can be supplied in blank form for those of you skilled in grinding. You can experiment and make your own profiles in the blank.

Resharpening

Carbide bits last five to ten times longer than steel between sharpenings. A typical carbide cutter with .090″ of carbide thickness can be reground four or five times if it hasn't suffered any catastrophic fractures.

A new bit is probably as sharp as it will ever be: 3-, 4- and 5-axis tool grinders in the factory are very expensive machines that grind in radial relief, the carbide faces and the bottoms of the flutes for good bottom cutting. No resharpening service is going to go to that much trouble, so don't expect the cutter to last as long on the regrind as it did when it was new. Nevertheless, in most cases a regrind will yield quite acceptable service. Grinding carbide is a sophisticated procedure and requires expensive factory machinery. High-speed steel can be sharpened in the small shop; carbide can't.

Figure 8-10
These two WKW cutters plunge straight through wood. The pointed boring end cutter is for through stock plunging and the other cutter is for blind flat-bottom work.

without sweeping the router. Solid carbide straight bits generally plunge whether spiral ground or straight fluted. Wisconsin Knife Works makes some carbide-faced bits with carbide boring points. They also are working on expanding the number of bottom-cutting bits to

Big Cutters

Small cutters, 1¾″ in diameter with less than 1½″ of flute length on ½″ shanks, are within the safe working range of router woodworking. Generally, work requiring larger cutters is best done with the analogous shaper cutter on the shaper. The shaper is not necessarily any safer than the router, but like the Indy 500 where certain types of driving are confined to those that can handle it in places designed for it, this type of machine work has its place.

Large router cutters, like firecrackers and guns, are readily available. The competition simply won't allow any one company exclusivity for large-diameter cutters. They are hazardous and require special attention. You should not consider using a cutter over 1¾″ in diameter unless you are well experienced. Panel raising, roundovers and other decorator bits are often 2″ to 4″ in diameter and can't safely be used in a hand router. Almost all of these large cutters are for outside use where only half the router will be on the work surface. When this much cutter is engaged in the workpiece there is simply too much opportunity for the tool to tip and rock, causing an accident. The router also has to start up with the cutter one radius or so away from the edge of stock. With a 3½″-diameter cutter in the collet, you'll have to start the router in the air rather than on the workpiece; something I'd rather not do. I do not recommend you hand rout—with or without an offset base—with cutters greater than 1¾″ in diameter.

These large cutters should only be used on the router table. The fence should hide most of the cutter and, due to the magnitude of the cut, it will have to be cut in stages. The use of these large cutters is beyond the scope of this text, and as I mentioned early on, some woodworking practices are acceptable but dangerous—this is one of them.

If the cuttings you desire require frequent use of large-diameter router bits you should buy a shaper. The shaper, with its large spindle, slow RPM and high power, can handily cut large profiles more safely than a router. Also, the multi-adjustable fences provided with shapers and their relatively large cast iron tables make the process more predictable and efficient. Prolonged large-diameter work on a router will kill the motor; a shaper hums with big cutters.

AVOIDING THE BROKEN BIT

The router bit industry knows there are those of us who would rather rout than hand-tool wood. They will even go so far as to make us cutters that they shouldn't, cutters that exceed sound engineering standards. Long, skinny straight bits (three or more times longer than the diameter of the shank), narrow-necked dovetail cutters, tiny veining or corebox bits, some keyhole cutters and most ¼″-shanked bits with very large cutting diameters (greater than 1⅝″) all fall into this fragile category (Figure 8-11).

Certain router approaches to woodworking problems are often out of the practical range of the routing process domain but they're done anyway. Box joints, some dovetails, narrow and deep mortises and long tenons, all possible with routers, probably should be sawn for the most part and not routed. Heavy-duty cuts like rabbeting, roundovers and other large trim cuts, to be done safely and efficiently, should be cut with the stronger ½″-shanked tools when possible, not with fragile ¼″-shanked tools (Figure 8-12).

Fragile cutters are a fact of life, however, and they can and will break from time to time. An outside, often bearing-guided, cutter is particularly dangerous when it breaks because it can go anywhere. An unpiloted bit doing inside work invariably, if it breaks, is confined to the pathway or excavation it is cutting. They don't usually go ballistic, they merely drop dead—and fairly rapidly, I might add. The router itself acts as a shield over the work site and traps the broken cutter below it.

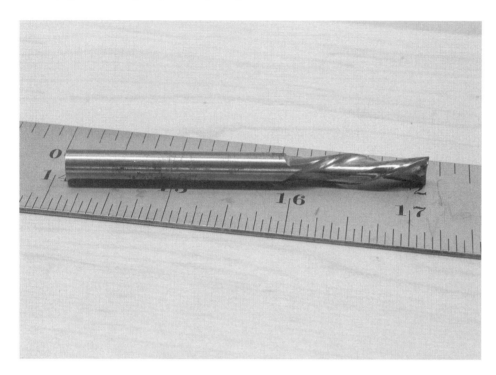

Figure 8-11A
This long straight bit will not, repeat, will not cut a chatter-free slot.

Figure 8-11B
The walls of these cuttings are chattered from these skinny bits. If you want the profile perfect and you have the time, you should use hand planes and molders to clean up the cut.

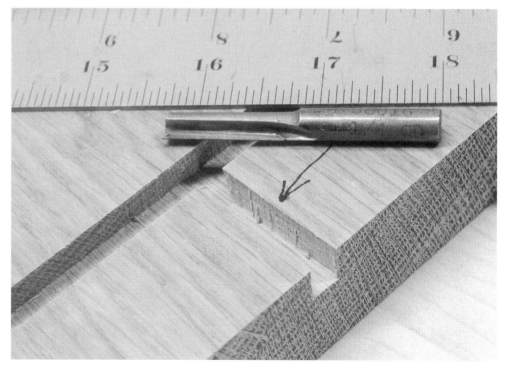

Figure 8-12
Both of these cutters are ⅜″ rabbet bits and they will cut equally well. However, I strongly advise the large-shanked models whenever possible. They are safer, cut better when worn and are less likely to break in adverse conditions.

Bit Safety Tips

My broken-bit experience has been lucky for me. All the narrow-necked cutters I've broken have stayed in their cuts and I've never broken a ¼″ piloted bit that hit me. The risk is there, however, and you may not be as lucky as I've been. My advice:

1. Never use a cutter indicated as "fragile" by the manufacturer or supplier.
2. Use ½″-shanked tools for piloted work even if it means you borrow or buy a ½″ router. (I've never broken a ½″-shank piloted bit. They're quite safe.)
3. Consider doing cuts that are out of the range of routing with hand tools or on the table saw, when practical.
4. Don't unleash an excessive length of cutter from the collet to get more depth of cut. Buy longer shanked tools and always keep at least ¾″ of shank in the collet.
5. When in doubt, take the cut in stages so as not to stress the daylights out of what little strength some of these cutters have.
6. Never rout unless you're comfortable with the cut.
7. If you're a daredevil be sure to wear as much protective gear as possible—including a plywood vest.

BIT STORAGE

Carbide tools are hard but, like glass, they chip and fracture. If you keep your cutters in the plastic pouch they come in they'll be safe, but not handy. I think you're more apt to use your stuff if you can see it, and surely if they're on display you won't have to sort through your envelopes to find what you're after. I use a 3″ × 2″ × 20″ glue-up with 33/64″ holes in it to store my bits. If you drill a couple of rows with a series of holes in each row, on 1½″ centers, most of your cutters won't bump into each other. I do keep any special bits in their pouches or in plastic medicine bottles.

CHAPTER NINE

Understanding the Router Table

The router table is an important element within the router province. In fact, a lot of the cuttings done with the portable tool can and should be done on the table. There are also some customary operations on the table that could be done a lot more safely and expeditiously with the hand router. For someone looking at the router table for the first time or for some of us reviewing what the table can do, it may not be clear just what the advantages and disadvantages are. It may be just as confusing deciding what the critical elements of a table router are. To be sure, routing on the router table is different than routing by hand; the skills are different and so are the safety considerations. I think you'll find as you read on that not only are the differences easily understood but the table itself can be quite simple to make and use.

THE ROUTER TABLE IS NOT A SHAPER

Routers and router tables are not necessarily production tools. They are designed for intermittent heavy-duty or continuous light-duty work. It would be a mistake to try and get the work from a router that a shaper can deliver. The hand circular saw and the table saw are similar in this respect. The router table and the hand router have traditionally and professionally been assistants to the shaper, not replacements for one. The router's smaller cutters, spindles, light duty and low cost fit in well where the shaper has gaps. Shapers are heavy-handed, with big motors and relatively slow speeds. Routers are light and high speed. The biggest spindle found in a common router is ½". The smallest spindle on a shaper is ½". Furthermore shaper spindles are sophisticated precision-ground components in vibration-free isolated assemblies, separate from their motors, with heavy-duty bearings. The router spindle is one and the same with the armature and performs double duty; their bearings are the first things to wear out. The router table does have one distinct advantage over the shaper, however, and that is the ability to do inside work.

Router tables are usually made of sheet metal, medium-density fiberboard (MDF) or plywood. Shaper tables are surface-ground cast iron with a whole complexity of precision-made machined parts and subassemblies. Shaper cutters are huge, 400 to 600 grams or more in weight and 3", 4" and 5" or more in diameter. Router bits are small, often 25 to 50 grams, with small diameters (Figure 9-1). Most router bits are less than 1⅝″ in diameter.

These grand differences suggest to me that the router table should exploit the strengths of the shaper that would best apply to the novelty of the router and not try to compete with it. And that is indeed the spirit in which this chapter is presented. (For more on the router table see: *The Router Table Book* by Ernie Conover, 1994, a Taunton Press publication.)

WORKPIECE PREPARATION

You can rout most of the same materials on the router table that you can by hand—except those materials that have to be climb cut, like aluminum. MDF (medium-density fiberboard), particle board, masonite, plywood, plastic, wallboard, many nonferrous metals, fiberglass, plastic laminate and other manmade materials can be routed on the router table. I might point out that these materials generally need little if any preparation to be routed, whereas wood should first visit the jointer, planer and table saw before meeting the router bit.

When table routing, the workpiece is in contact with a lot of the table's two control surfaces (the fence and the top) before it arrives at the cutter. A portable router at most has 5″ to 7″ of contact with the workpiece. The shape of the work, then, is far more important when working on the router table. If the workpiece is poorly dimensioned but flat on all sides it can be satisfactorily table routed. The results can and will be

Figure 9-1
This heavy-duty straight shaper cutter dwarfs its router bit counterpart.

confusing, however, since poorly dimensioned means nonuniform in thickness and width, as well as being out of square. Decorative cuts are usually relatively forgiving of poorly dimensioned material, but some cuts can be quite dangerous and others of such a consequence as to be useless. Joints will not fit if produced from tapered stock, and cuts on squares, for example, can rock against the fence, kick back and jam the cutter.

Misshapen workpieces that are well dimensioned are just as hazardous. It is possible, for instance, to avoid the jointer and plane unflattened stock. You can also, given the power and perhaps a power feeder, saw uniformly and cut off square. Industry does it every day. Stock that is crooked, bowed, cupped, twisted or otherwise screwed up can be machined quite accurately—but not on the router table. The router table can tolerate gentle bow, and even that at times can be a problem. Contorted wood will give you variable results, and since so many router bits are deeply engaged in the workpiece the risk of kickback is high, especially if you should relax your hold-down forces—even for a second.

Contorted and poorly dimensioned lumber, like drinking and driving, is the cause of far more accidents with experienced woodworkers than flat-dimensioned stock in the hands of amateurs. If you expect professional results in your woodworking, you will either have to have control of the material or you'll have to pay somebody to do it for you. You cannot achieve crisp joinery, unfuzzed decoration or satisfactory millings from obnoxious material that is poorly dimensioned. Furthermore, your tools wear out sooner and you will always be at some risk. Given well-prepared stock, then, what workpieces are best managed on the router table?

Small Workpieces

The router table, with its inverted motor and adjustable fence, is ideal for small workpieces too difficult to clamp and rout portably. However, if there is any danger of the workpiece jamming in either the cutter hole or the fence, then the workpiece will have to be fixtured or the fence modified (Figure 9-2). A carrier or vacuum template may help, as may clamping the workpiece to a

Figure 9-2

This narrow ⅞″ square stick is small enough to steer into the cutter opening in the fence. It should be routed on a longer piece and then cut to net length.

jig, fixture or another piece of wood (Figures 9-3 and 9-4). A specialized fence that just fits the cutter will keep the workpiece from steering into the fence (Figure 9-5). A curved fence will facilitate the routing of disks and wheels (Figure 9-6) too small to hand rout. You may also want to rout a large workpiece and then harvest the profile off the slab rather than rout the profile on skinny stock (Figure 9-7).

With so many options in workpiece han-dling, there is just no excuse for risking an in-jury. Don't rout if you feel threatened; it's sim-ply not worth it. There's usually a way to do it safely. Incidentally, I don't rout anything I can't hold well with two hands.

How Big?

A workpiece can be table routed on end (stand-ing up), on its edge and on its face. In each of

Figure 9-3

You can do some cutting on the end of this stick if you clamp it to another workpiece. It won't tear out if it's clamped evenly and securely.

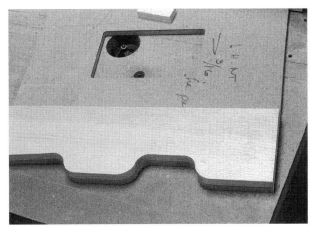

Figure 9-4

I screwed this workpiece to the much larger template for its profile.

Figure 9-5

I clamped this board onto my fence and then pivoted it into the cutter. It forms its own shape in the fence, just as if it were clay. If you have a spare, perhaps cosmetically compromised, cutter of the same or nearly the same shape, use it to form the pocket. You can burn a cutter out doing this.

Figure 9-6

A curved fence like this that matches the radius of the disk is an excellent way to rout. The cutter is completely covered up and the work is always well supported.

Figure 9-7
A safe way to rout narrow tambors is to rout them on a large, safesize plank and then rip them off on the table saw. Have we transferred the danger of routing to the dangers in ripping narrow stock? I hope not. I ripped these on the band saw.

these positions there are at least two routable surfaces. For example, if a 10″ × 12″ × ¾″ workpiece is flat on the table, any one of its four edges can be routed (a slot perhaps) or the fence and cutter can be adjusted to cut the face (a rabbet). If you can pass the workpiece by the cutter (motor off) for its full length of cut, it is routable. If you can pass and press the workpiece continuously and uniformly by the cutter and not have it squiggle, you can rout it well. It is unfortunate, however, that in the second case the results can be less than desirable even though you're in control. Nonetheless, I can say unequivocally that if you can't execute the second scenario your results will always be less than desirable.

Wood is a strange material. Sometimes it must be backed up with stock to keep it from tearing out. It routs differently across the grain, down the grain or on a radius. The same cut you had success with one day may be a problem the next. The same cut on a large workpiece can split a small one. To get good results most of the time requires a lot of practice and good to excellent control of the work. It is possible, in my opinion, to fixture most any cut so that the results are predictable and acceptable. The setup can also be arranged so that it is safe. It can be

extraordinarily difficult, but most fixturing is relatively easy to do (Figure 9-8). You must accept the fact that good results, good fixturing and safety are all interrelated and can be inversely proportional to time. It is often the case that I'll spend an hour or more on setup and jigging and only seconds on the cut.

Routing on the table often requires jigging

Figure 9-8
Here I've set up for an open-ended mortise. The stop on the outfeed side of the fence will stop all the boards in the same place. The three ¼″-thick slabs of plastic elevate the workpiece so I don't have to make depth of cut changes. After each pass I remove one thickness of plastic.

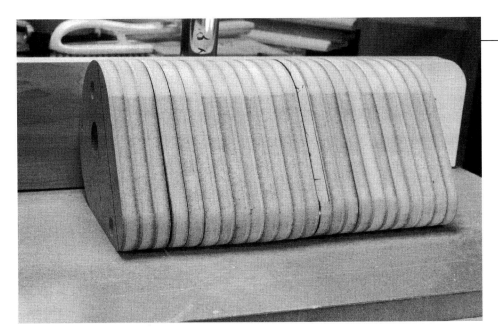

Figure 9-9
Whenever you have a lot of equal or similar parts that need the same operation, the router table should be considered. This stack of templates in need of "easy edges" is a perfect example.

and fixturing; large workpieces less so than small ones. For material that is straight-line routed off the fence (noncurved stock), the size and weight limitations are related to balance and control. If your router table tips over with the heaviest workpiece you can heft that's one limitation; another relates to length and weight. If the workpiece is too heavy and long and you don't have the strength to hold it down for the full length of cut that's another limitation. Common sense and safety should be your guidelines. For me, flat work up to about 20 lbs. is all I can handle. My 2′ × 2′ table and me will support about 7 feet of stock (under 20 lbs.). An extension table can assist, but generally if I have to call on an extension I'll rout the piece by hand. Most workpieces that have to be end routed (tenoned, for example) are best done fixtured with the hand router. There's simply no practical way to rout a tenon on the end of an 80″ bed rail on the router table—or a 4′ table rail, for that matter.

The Ideal Workpiece

The easiest workpieces to rout are no longer than about two times the length of your table. They are light and small enough to slide along the table and fence without teetering.

Rails, stiles, legs and drawer parts are best table routed. Stuff that needs an "easy" or decorative edge, like shelving, plaques and picture frame parts, are easy to rout. Long grain is much easier to rout than cross grain, and it doesn't need to be backed up to prevent tearout. Stopped long-grain cuts like open-ended mortises and dovetail slots on legs and stiles are also well suited for table routing. Production cuttings are almost always done more expeditiously on the table, since the mess is easy to collect, no clamping is needed and the handling is simplified (Figure 9-9).

ADVANTAGES OF TABLE ROUTING

There are some real advantages to using the router table. Some of the advantages are setup related, others relate to efficiency and some are just accidents of the design. For example, a router table can, by virtue of its enclosure, be very quiet. If the motor is surrounded by a cabinet, with a door for access, the noise can be so low that you can speak over it without raising your voice. Another advantage is that the table is always ready for work. It is a workstation in its own right. To use a portable router you need to clear off a bench, find some clamps and hunt down the extension cord. For most table work all you need to do is adjust the fence and turn on the motor. The surface is dedicated.

The Hidden Cutter

The inverted router, in most cases, hides and protects us from the cutter. Router table work is largely fractional edge work and not usually full-thickness cuts. What that means is the cutter is covered up by the work. As a rule it is not safe to cut on the top of the work, since any variation in thickness or contortion in the board could jam the cutter and kick back the workpiece (Figure 9-10). There is also some danger at the end of the cut, as the cutter may appear unexpectedly and startle you. You must prepare to have your hands out of harm's way or use push sticks. On balance, the hidden cutter is more of a safety benefit than its sudden appearance is a risk.

Figure 9-10

If you cut on top of the workpiece like this, there is risk of kickback, especially if the board is poorly dimensioned or otherwise contorted.

Unpiloted Bits

Bearing cutters can be used on the router table, but I usually don't. If I'm straight-line routing the fence is my guide, not a bearing. Bearings are useful and sometimes mandatory for curved work, but most table work is done on the straight sides of a workpiece up against the fence.

There are a couple of reasons I rarely use piloted bits on the router table; the first is economic. Unpiloted bits, especially straight cutters, are cheaper than analogous bearing-guided rabbet bits—and I don't have to replace a bearing on a cutter that doesn't have one.

The second reason I don't use bearings on the router table is that edge defects transfer. If you are using a pilot bearing against a less than perfect edge, every defect will transfer to the profile. Moreover, it's usually the case that the frequency of the edge joint defects are such that they cause minor resonances ("bearing bounce"). These vibrations usually work-harden the edge and produce a chattered profile (Figure 9-11). Frequently these defects can be sanded out, but they don't occur when a fence has been used. A straight, square fence can more than average out the edge defects. And if the workpiece and fence are really straight the cuttings are better than the edges they're produced from—a real plus. If you must use a bearing-guided bit on straight work, adjust the fence so the bearing is out of play (Figure 9-12).

Depths of Cut

There are two depths of cut to be attended to on the table. A lot of portable cuttings are bearing piloted, so the side to side depth of cut is automatically accounted for; a ⅜″ rabbet bit, for example, cuts ⅜″ laterally. On the table the fence takes the place of the bearing for edge and inside

Figure 9-11

The sample on the bottom was cut off the fence while the one on top was cut using a bearing. The edge defects on the sample cut off the fence did not transfer to the profile.

Figure 9-12

With a stick and a .005" feeler gauge I can set the fence so the bearing is out of play.

work and therefore requires adjustment. The cutter height also has to be set. Both of these adjustments are easy and conspicuous, though some would argue that the cutter height adjustment is problematic. The continuous adjustability (not in increments, like bearings) of the fence is a distinct advantage, pretty much exclusive to table routing.

If the cutter design will allow it, the lateral depth of cut can be adjusted from nothing to more than a cutter diameter. That is especially desirable when making an odd-size rabbet with a straight bit, say $^{13}/_{64}"$ or $^{27}/_{32}"$. You can also get more mileage out of certain cutters by adjusting the extension of an unused section of a cutter into the playground (Figure 9-13). V-groove and chamfer bits, for example, produce the same bevels on any section of their flutes. If a cutter whose bottom third of flute is spent is adjusted so the upper two-thirds are in play, you can double or triple the service of the tool before resharpening. Not all tools are so friendly, especially if the bit had a bearing on it or for some other reason may only cut one radius.

Variable Workpiece Approach

A board can be fed to the cutter on a router table on any of its six surfaces. If the surface has insufficient contact with either the fence or the top it might have to be fixtured for the trip

Figure 9-13

The upper section (near the shank) of this 45° cutter has never touched a piece of wood. The bottom third of the cutter (near the bearing) has been worn out cutting laminate. I can adjust the fence and cutter height to use that section of the cutter, something you can't do with the portable router and bearing.

Figure 9-14

I just can't tenon the faces on the end of this stick safely. There simply isn't enough stock in contact with the control surfaces (the fence and top).

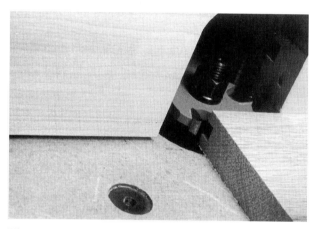

Figure 9-15

I can slot rout the edge of this board without any handling problems.

Figure 9-16

The same board can be cut along its face (work on edge) with no changes in setup or handling problems.

(Figure 9-14). In those instances, it may be just as easy or even more practical to rout the profile with the handheld router. In those instances where there are no handling problems (Figures 9-15 and 9-16, for example), the router table can be particularly more efficacious to table rout than hand rout. One of the ways I can demonstrate this is with the use of a slotter.

A drawer side should be slotted to receive a drawer bottom. A slotter is the most efficient tool to form a groove near the edge (usually no more than 1½″ from the edge) of a board (Figure 9-17). It is very difficult to rout the slot by hand, since the edge of the board presents so little surface to the router. On the router table the fence provides the support and the cut is really easy to do. To slot the edge (long grain or end grain), either approach is easy but the table rout requires no clamping or ball bearing and is simply more efficient.

The use of any one cutter can be expanded, too, depending on how you present the work to

Figure 9-17

All the cuttings to make this laminated section were done with just one ¼″-thick slotter. These great little tools cut up to ⁹⁄₁₆″ deep and there are at least a dozen thicknesses to choose from. Almost all the table saw slot cuts you're used to can be done on the router table with slotters.

Figure 9-18

The two cuttings produced on this stick are from the same 60° cutter set to the same depth of cut.

Figure 9-19

The conventional ogee is cut with the workpiece flat on the table. The other cut is done with the workpiece on edge at the same depth of cut.

Figure 9-20

All these cuts were done with just one straight bit on the router table (notch, groove and tongue).

the cutter. A 60° chamfer bit can produce a 30° cut on edge (Figure 9-18). An ogee presents two remarkably different profiles just by passing the work on edge or on "the flat" at the same depth of cut (Figure 9-19). A solitary straight bit can groove, dado, notch or tongue just by changing the depth of cut and the position of the fence (Figure 9-20). There are countless examples of this idiosyncrasy; try to exploit it whenever you can.

TABLE ACCESSORIES

A handheld router is a concentration of stuff—very different from a router table, which is quite spread out. The workpiece, when hand routed with other than a bearing-guided cutter, will require a tool guide, perhaps a stop and some means of holding the work. The workpiece on the router table is free to slide along the fence and top unencumbered. Many times it is far easier to fixture a cut on the router table than it is on the workpiece. A stop on the fence, a hold-down or a back-up block are all examples. Usually, if the best choice is to table rout, the fixturing is relatively easy. Curved, template and pin routing tasks on the table are another matter, but for general cabinet and furniture making the fixturing is straightforward.

The Miter Gauge

The miter gauge is a useful accessory if you do a lot of end-grain work on narrow stock (Figure 9-21), such as door stiles and drawer parts. The tool is excellent for transporting the stock past the cutter, but all through-end-grain cuts tear out as the part leaves the cutter. A backing block is essential for miter gauge work too. If you use a miter tool (with its blade in a slot) in

Figure 9-21

I use a miter gauge so infrequently that I've never cut a slot in the table for it. I just use two ³⁄₈"-thick pieces of MDF to trap the blade, and I can always get the travel parallel to the fence this way.

Figure 9-22

The vacuum manifold on my fence is made of plastic and wood. It ain't perfect, but it's acceptable. A wide workpiece passing by and covering up the cutter hole will be sucked against the fence. I think this is helpful in keeping the work tight against the fence but it can surprise you.

conjunction with the fence, you'll have to adjust the fence so it's parallel to the miter slot. This in turn makes the net fence adjustment difficult because its distance from the cutter centerline and the parallelism to the slot are often in conflict. Quality work can be achieved but the setup may be a bit tedious. Incidentally, end-grain cutting requires a lot of power and consequently a lot of force on your part. If door work is common or if you are considering light commercial work, you should use a shaper. Shaper cutters last a lot longer, there is a far greater selection of profiles

and the machine won't burn out from this relatively abusive task.

Vacuum Collection

Routing seems to be the messiest woodworking operation there is. Most portable routing messes are uncollectible. Though Skil-Bosch and DeWalt have engineered some excellent collectors for their portable routers, the overwhelming number of portable routers are used without dust collection. I often choose the router table over the hand-held router just because I can collect the mess. Both the router and the shaper produce substantial messes, but at a concentrated source that is easy to collect. My fence has a chamber behind the cutter to which I installed a 1½″ tube (Figure 9-22) for my vacuum. My system is not perfect but it is acceptable. Mess from inside work (e.g., dados), which I don't usually do on the table, is uncollectible with my system. You can, however, design ducting, etc., to collect from under the table to render inside cuts clean. Chip-collecting accessories for the router fence can be found in some router bit catalogs (CMT Tools, MLCS, Woodhaven) and woodworking tool catalogs.

Porter Cable has recently entered the vacuum competition with a 10-amp, 9-gallon Italian import. The unit fits neatly right under and inside my router table (Figure 9-23). The machine is equipped with an electronic-sensitive power outlet that automatically turns on the vacuum when I start the router (Figure 9-24). The tool also has a 25′ extension cord, so finding a power outlet is never a problem. The vacuum automatically shuts off 15 seconds after you shut of the router—at last, a user friendly tool.

Figure 9-23
By chance, this Porter Cable vacuum fits exactly beneath and inside the confines of my router table.

Figure 9-24
This vacuum has an integral power outlet that automatically turns on the vacuum when I turn on the router. The hose is long enough (13′) to be used for floor clean-up and other power tools without having to move the power unit.

CHAPTER TEN
Safety and the Router Table

Safety and the use of the router table are intimately related. A cut that is awkward, torn out, burnt or otherwise less than acceptable is usually done at risk. Good cuttings are just as likely to be safe cuttings. Most or all of the safety precautions listed in chapter five, also apply to table routing. There are, however, some special precautions I'd like you to know about.

SECURE THE FENCE

Since the fence is almost always in play, some provision must be made to secure it well. If it slips the cut will be spoiled and the work could be kicked back. I always push on the fence at least as hard as I expect to push on the workpiece before I rout to make sure it won't slip. C-clamp it down and clamp a board behind the fence if you think it might move (Figure 10-1).

The fence should hide the cutter as much as possible. If the window for the cutter in the fence is designed for your largest cutter, like mine is, it may be too big for a small cutter. A short workpiece could rotate into the window and kick back. In those cases where there is some risk, I'll screw on or clamp on an auxiliary fence that is custom shaped for the cutter (see Figure 9-5).

Figure 10-1
The carrier member of my fence is bolted to the table with two ⁵⁄₁₆"-18 cap screws, but it still can move. If you clamp a stick behind your fence like this it will be secure, and you can reference off of it.

WATCH BIG CUTTERS

Big cutters, like big guns, look scary. They are manageable, but for those of you just starting out they can be dangerous—especially if you are working off their bearings on curved or straight pieces. If the work is curved, the cutter is probably totally exposed and the fence is out of play. The more a tool bit is unguarded the greater the

Figure 10-2
Any old stick can be used as a fulcrum point. You should have two clamps on it, however, to keep it from slipping.

chance for an injury. Moreover, a free-handed piece on a bearing cutter is risky to rout because the start of the cut can throw the workpiece back at you. A fulcrum of some sort (Figure 10-2), can make the start easier and safer, but there is still risk and a certain amount of skill is mandatory. If you're hell-bent on routing curved parts with big cutters, get your feet wet with small cutters first (Figures 10-3 and 10-4).

Big cutters are normally run at slower speeds since there is some risk of imbalance and they burn stock at the higher speeds. As a cutter runs slower than its maximum speed of efficiency, part of the work (task) is shifted to the operator; you have to hold down and push harder. Using a big cutter already has some risk due to its size, exposure and proximity to your hands. You know when you rout, joint or shape your feed forces have to be near or concentrated toward the cutter head to be effective. This is especially pronounced on curved cuts done without a fence. Now, if you run the cutter slow you have the added burden of higher hand-feed forces, so the risk is heightened. Nevertheless, be especially careful using big cutters, and whenever possible use a workpiece holder that keeps your hands as far from the cutter as possible.

Figure 10-3
A small cutter like this roundover bit is a good tool to learn bearing-guided work on the table.

Figure 10-4
A plastic guard over the cutter offers some protection, but keep your hands at a distance nonetheless.

BE CAREFUL USING THE CLIMB CUT

For most work on the router table you have no choice but to feed right to left on edge cuts (Figure 10-5). As you may have guessed, this anti-climb feed will cause some tear-out. Sharp cutters, light cuts and good wood will help, but there will be times when there is nothing you can do but watch your stock tear out right in front of you. If it is absolutely essential that the work not tear out you can hand rout in a climb cut. The climb cut done by hand is manageable with due caution, experience and light cuts. The climb cut on the router table can be extremely hazardous.

The climb cut (feed left to right) on the table can unexpectedly pull the workpiece right out of your hand, because the feed direction is with the cutter rotation. The workpiece will be a mess and, more tragically, you can be eaten alive by the cutter. The transfer of power from the cutter to the workpiece is far more influential on the table than with the hand held router; the smaller the workpiece the greater the power transfer.

Moreover, as you climb cut your ability to feed the stock diminishes because the tool bit forces the workpiece away from the fence, and therefore the depth of cut varies. This variable depth of cut results in an intermittent and jerky feed, which sooner or later will cause you to lose your grip on the work. Then off goes the work and if you're lucky you don't pull back a stub.

There is a remarkable difference in handling between the climb and anti-climb cuts on the table. The anti-climb cut pulls the workpiece against the fence and pushes the work back at you fairly uniformly; the force is relatively constant and natural. The climb cut is exactly the opposite. The workpiece is constantly being pulled from you, not pushed at you, and driven away from the fence. These phenomena are unexpected, variable and unnatural. The climb cut with the hand router transfers a lot of the excess power into 10 or 15 lbs. of a router that is quite inertial. The router absorbs the energy and you and the tool are under far more control. This is not the case on the table, especially with ordinary workpieces, which are much lighter than a router. (A cabinet door stile weighs about 1 lb.

Figure 10-5
I put this big arrow on my fence so my students and I don't forget the safe way to feed.

and a ⅝″-thick drawer side 6″×18″ might only weigh 1½ lbs.)

Very light climb cuts on the table are permissible if they do not have any tendency to pull the workpiece out of your hands; an ⅛″×45° bevel, for instance. The workpiece should be large enough to protect from the cutter; narrow short pieces are always suspect. A power feeder can be used, if applied correctly, for most climb cuts, but that technology is the subject of another book.

The Accidental Climb Cut

When I table rout on the inside of stock (a dovetail slot or open mortise for example), I always use a single cutter-width cut.

That is, if I want a ½″ groove I use a ½″ cutter, not two passes from a ¼″ cutter. You will be at risk if you widen a slot on the wrong side of the cut with straight bits. The cut may actually be a climb cut, even though you are feeding from right to left (Figure 10-6). I strongly advise you to find a way to center your cuts, and whenever possible to adjust the tongues and tenons to fit the anatomy of single cutter-width slots rather than widening them. (A slotter can widen at no risk; Figure 10-7.) Climb cutting is hazardous and is always associated with some element of risk.

BEWARE OF SHARP EDGES

The crisp edges of the router-cut workpiece are more of a hazard on the router table than when they are produced by the hand-fed router. Obviously, if you're handling the work you're more apt to get sliced than you are when your hands are on the rounded handles of a router. Tearout, a much more common occurrence on the

Figure 10-6
You're looking at the outfeed side of the tunnel on this workpiece. If the feed is right to left and you're widening the tunnel on the fence side, say "goodbye" to the workpiece. The workpiece can be fed left to right safely, however. Try and match the cutter to the slot to avoid this ambiguity.

Figure 10-7
A radially designed slotter like this can be used to widen a slot at no risk. The feed is from right to left.

Figure 10-8
Cutting on the top side of a workpiece like this traps the workpiece between the cutter and top. A defective board can easily be kicked back at you in this configuration.

Figure 10-9
This condition traps the workpiece between the cutter and the fence. The same thing happens when you're widening a slot. In either case, any contortion of the board or errors in feed may jam the work, kick it back and/or cause an injury. Don't do it.

table, is also more likely to sticker you. Be prepared for this, especially if you rout both faces of the stock.

THE SMALL WORKPIECE STRANGENESS FACTOR

A small workpiece, a door or drawer pull for example, is far more subject to splitting than a large workpiece from the same cutter and depth of cut. A large workpiece has a lot of material to absorb the cutting forces of a speeding router bit. A minor check or split in a big workpiece may pass the cutter unnoticed. The same defect in a small workpiece can be the nucleus for a compound fracture. A split can also occur even if the part is sound. I discovered this early on when I fixtured a narrow door pull to a template with screws. On the first break I assumed I may have overstressed the work with the screws. The second time it happened, like the first, on the end grain on a very clear piece of straight-grained material. It has subsequently happened so many times at random that I'm convinced that the small workpiece is plumb easier to

break—and it does. Be aware and protect yourself with workpiece holders, hold-downs or light cuts. Given this scenario, you may not want to rout small parts at all. I don't. My strategy now is to band saw and sand. There are times when routing is simply not a smart thing to do.

PREVENT KICKBACK

Kickback is far more common on the router table than on the bench. One of the reasons for this is that a defective stick often has its greatest influence on its long centerline when the part is fully engaged in the cut. A bowed workpiece with a straight cutter in it will be less handleable when it springs back. On the long centerline (halfway down the stick) the cutter may start to cut more on one side of cutter than the other. It is at this moment that the workpiece is most likely to kick back. Defective, poorly dimensioned stock or cuttings where a lot of material is being wasted are conditions subject to kickback. A lot of workpiece is already on the table and up against the fence by the time it reaches the cutter, so defects are more maleficent than when they are hand routed. There are also more kickback-favorable opportunities on the table, such as bit trapping and cutting on the top side of the workpiece (Figures 10-8 and 10-9).

BE CAREFUL MAKING FULL-THICKNESS CUTS

Full-thickness cuts on the router table require an adjustable outfeed fence. As a rule, full-thickness cuts are industrial-strength cuts and should be done on a shaper; light template cuts are the exceptions (Figure 10-10). If your cuts nearly take the full thickness of stock you're routing you could be at risk. I make it a point to leave at least ⅛″ against the fence on most profiles (Figure 10-11) for safety. The less material against the fence, the greater its chance of deformation or breakage resulting in injury or kickback. Occasional full-thickness cuts are done safely with the hand router and template. If *occasionally* turns into *all the time*, get a shaper.

MAKING STOPPED CUTS

Stopped cuts like on an open mortise (Figure 10-12) are pretty safe on well cared for material. The cuts here are open to the cutter on one end and not excessively tunneled into the work; a 2″- to 4″-long open dovetail slot is a good example. I would never drop a workpiece onto a spinning cutter for a blind-ended cut. Although this practice is textbook acceptable, it is dangerous and you should not do it. The cuttings I've seen done in this way are usually borderline to unacceptable. Crummy cuttings are usually done at some risk to either you or the workpiece. A safer approach would call for a fixtured workpiece and a portable plunge router.

Figure 10-10
This template-assisted cut is a full-thickness cut but I've band sawn it such that only a ¹⁄₁₆″ or so is being routed. Heavy, full-thickness cuts are for the shaper.

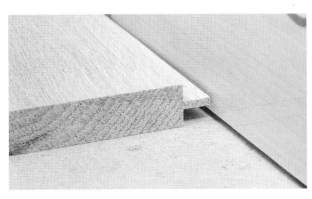

Figure 10-11
I've formed a skinny tongue on the work by rabbeting an equal amount from both faces. I like to leave at least an ⅛″ of material against the fence for safety.

Figure 10-12
This dovetail (stopped mortise) was preceded by a series of straight bit cuts. Even a big dovetail bit like this might break off if thrust into a workpiece without a pre-routed tunnel. If you wobble the work, you'll tear the walls of the pathway, burn the profile or kick back the work.

CHAPTER ELEVEN

A Simple Router Table

The basic components of the router table are the stand, the work surface and the fence. The stand should be at the best working height for you. It should be stable and unlikely to tip over. If the motor compartment is paneled with ¾″-thick particle board or MDF a 2′×2′×35″ high stand will weigh 50 to 60 pounds. Add a 15 lb. router, a ¾″ thick MDF top and a fence and you'll probably have 85 to 100 lbs. This is enough mass for most jobs, but it's not easy to move around. You should have a handy and remote motor switch on your side of the table, one that you can't accidentally start, but near enough to switch off quickly in an emergency (Figure 11-1). There is nothing critical about the stand, but when you fasten the top to it make sure it doesn't distort the top.

You may want to make a cabinet out of your router stand, with doors, drawers, shelves and other components, but I'd advise against it. I regard the router table as I do any good stationary, and just as I couldn't see shelves beneath a planer or a table saw, I can't see them under a router table. A first-generation stand might consist of just four kiln-dried softwood 2×4s as legs and ¾″-thick panels tongued and grooved into each (Figure 11-2). Corner braces, whether metal or wood, would be worth the trouble. A window or only half a panel should be on one

Figure 11-1

I routed out a window on the side near the front of the stand for the switch. The toggle is out of reach for an accidental start, but pretty handy nonetheless.

side of the stand for the access to the motor. (The next grade up would have both floor and top rails; Figure 11-3.) Some provision should be made to attach the top. At a minimum, glue and screw some predrilled 1½″ square cleats, to the top inside face of the panels. Through these cleats attach the top. You may screw through the top into the cleats, as it may be too difficult through the cabinet. Your stand is crude, cheap, reasonably heavy and ugly, but a good first edi-

Using L[...]

A plastic la[...]
to rout on[...]
plied well.[...]
minus .005[...]
laminate h[...]
importantl[...]
how well c[...]
at it you m[...]
Both faces[...]
might say t[...]
there are n[...]
ment appli[...]
surface flat[...]
may wind[...]
what you s[...]
slightly bu[...]
However, i[...]
cope and s[...]
you might[...]
traced to a[...]
torted surf[...]
can screw[...]

MDF is[...]
or Minwax[...]
raw MDF[...]
faces (using[...]
been using[...]
now with l[...]
(Figure 11-[...]

The Cu[...]

It's hard to[...]
Some prefe[...]
You may u[...]
which case[...]
closer to y[...]
iment with[...]
cheap, so i[...]
much.

tion. Make the second edition based on what you don't like about this one. It's not a bad approach to jig and fixture making—besides, you'll never get exactly what you want the first time anyway.

THE MOTOR AND THE TOP

In my view, there is only one choice in routers for the router table. Router table work is almost always anti-climb (feed direction against the cutter rotation); you should feed the stock from right to left as you face the work side of the fence. As you feed the stock (right to left), the cutter takes the full profile because the work is

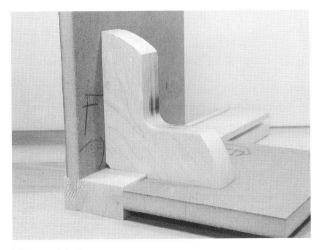

Figure 11-2
This corner is a simple, spartan, ugly but durable construction example for a router table. The corner brace will add a lot of rigidity.

Figure 11-3A
My present router table has four floor and four top rails. There are two more rails under the top.

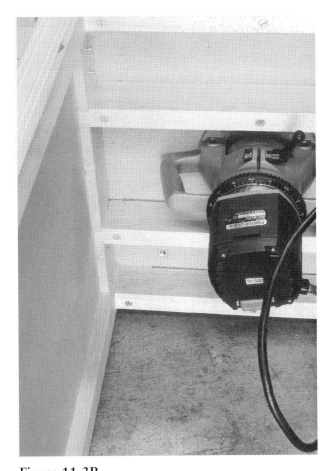

Figure 11-3B
I fastened the top to the upper six rails with long 1/4"-20 flathead bolts. The MDF is threadable and each hole has indeed been tapped.

pulled into
with any pr
goes to the
demand is l
so each pas
profile, and
is no choice
table cuts a
quire a lot o
the power, .
tained all-d:
abuse. The
should be b
more on thi
is the strong
chined flat.
top helps ke
into the slat
tend to dist

The case
thickness of
attached, w:

intersect you'll have the bolt hole pattern (Figure 11-6). Now, if you drill four equally spaced ¹¹/₃₂″ countersunk holes on the circle you can fasten the casting to the top. Use 1″ × ⁵/₁₆″-18 flathead screws for the assembly. If you're using another router you can use the base plate to transfer the hole pattern. Remember now when you're applying the battens to locate them so they don't interfere with the casting.

The Fence

Now that you have a stand and a work surface, all you need is a fence. My fence and one I'd recommend to you is a simple two-stage pivot fence. It incorporates a pivotal microadjust section mounted on a slotted member, the carrier. The fence carrier slots in cahoots with two pairs of T-nuts in the table top allow about 5″ of rough travel. The microadjust travel range is about the same as the range of cutter diameters I use, from about ½″ to 2″, or about 1½″ (Figure 11-7).

The pivotal element of the fence is in a T sec-

tion because that design tends to keep the face flat and straight. The horizontal member of the T also provides the secondary function, with its slot, of microadjustment without interfering with the vertical member. Let's separate out the parts and make one.

BUILDING THE CARRIER

STEP 1 Cut a 7″ × ⅞″ thick piece of hardwood (or ¾″-thick MDF) to 24″ in length.

STEP 2 Rout two ⁵/₁₆″ × 2½″ long slots centered on the workpiece on 11½″ centers. Stop the slots 1⅜″ from the back edge. The rough positioning of the fence is facilitated by these slots. If you don't mind C-clamping the fence in its rough position, then the slotting in this step is unnecessary.

STEP 3 The remaining work on the carrier requires the pivot fence assembly in hand, so let's start on it.

Figure 11-4

A couple of c
casting will k
with the wor

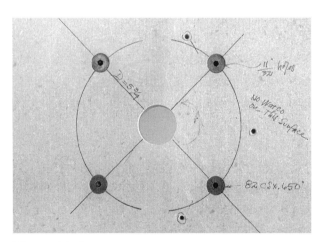

Figure 11-6
Two intersecting lines at 90° on a 5¾″ circle indicate the hole centers for a 7518 Porter Cable base casting. The holes should be ¹¹/₃₂″ and countersunk on the work face.

Figure 11-7
The fence can pivot about 1½″. At the maximum point of travel the lock bolt is no longer in the slot. If you need more travel than that, make the horizontal member wider.

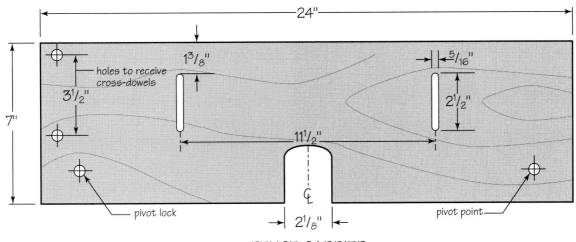

FENCE CARRIER

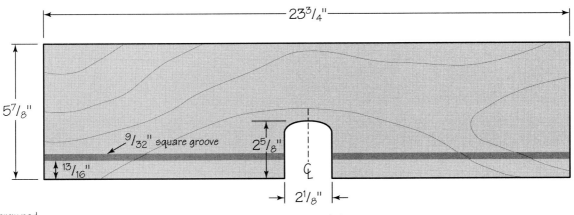

FENCE FACE

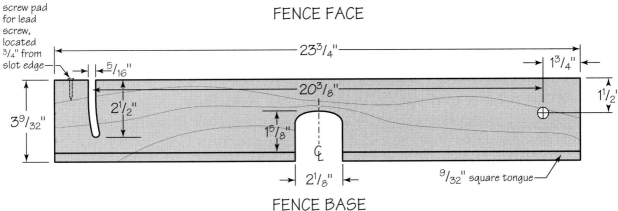

FENCE BASE

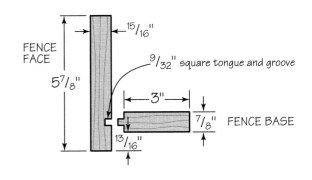

Materials Required

Carrier—⁷⁄₈″ × 7″ × 24″ hardwood (or ¾″ MDF)

Face—¹⁵⁄₁₆″ × 5⅞″ × 23¾″ hardwood

Base—⁷⁄₈″ × 3⁹⁄₃₂″ × 23¾″ hardwood

BUILDING THE PIVOTAL FENCE

(¾" MDF is an acceptable alternate material)

STEP 1 Cut one 3⁵⁄₁₆" × ⅞" straight-grained piece of hardwood to 23¾".

STEP 2 Cut one 5⅞" × ⅞" piece of hardwood to 23¾".

STEP 3 Template rout, band saw or jigsaw a centered 2⅝" × 2⅛" wide window out of the bottom part of the vertical fence member.

STEP 4 Cut a corresponding window out of the narrow (horizontal) member, but only 1⅝" deep.

STEP 5 Bore a ⁵⁄₁₆" hole in the horizontal member as shown. This is the pivot point.

STEP 6 Make a 20⅜" pivot arm for your plunge router (Figure 11-8), and rout a curved slot as shown. A ⁷⁄₁₆" straight slot centered at 20⅜" from the pivot center will also work.

STEP 7 Position the bottom of the horizontal member parallel and ¹³⁄₁₆" from the bottom edge of the vertical member and screw them together. Use 2" no. 12 flat-head sheet metal screws every 2½" to 3½" to secure. If you have tongue and groove skills, form a ⁹⁄₃₂" square centered tongue on the horizontal piece. The corresponding slot should be positioned on the vertical member so that on assembly there is ¹³⁄₁₆" of space beneath it and the bottom edge of the vertical member.

STEP 8 Assemble the pivotal section of the fence.

POSITIONING THE FENCE ON THE CARRIER

STEP 1 Center the fence on the carrier lengthwise (don't cover up the slots). Keep the slotted (outfeed) end against the edge of the carrier but separate the pivot end from the carrier by ⅜". This tactic will keep the fence from binding while pivoting.

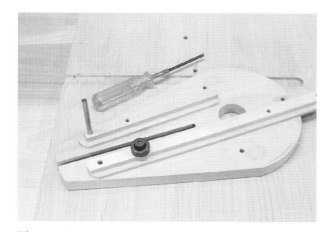

Figure 11-8
This circle-cutting jig is fully adjustable. You needn't make such a jig to cut the arc. You can use 6" × 30" × ⅜" thick MDF with a pivot hole drilled 20⅜" centered from the cutter.

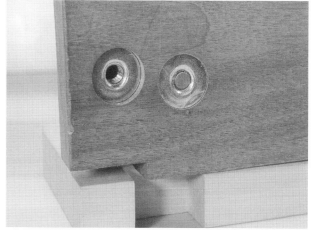

Figure 11-9
T-nuts will never pull through the stock; a threaded insert might. The flange of the nut should be countersunk.

Figure 11-10A

I cut, drilled and machined these aluminum brackets to 90°. They work nicely as fence reinforcements.

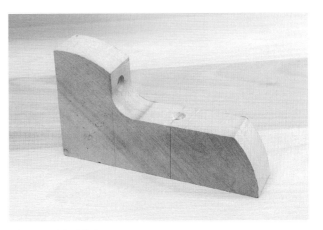

Figure 11-10B

A wooden corner brace is a lot easier to make.

STEP 2 Once the fence is located, clamp it on the carrier and use a ⁵⁄₁₆″ transfer punch or ⁵⁄₁₆″ brad point drill to mark the holes for the pivot and lever lock.

STEP 3 Drill the carrier at these punch marks for ⁵⁄₁₆″-18 T-nuts. Install the nuts on the bottom of the carrier. Rosan or equivalent ⁵⁄₁₆″-18 threaded inserts can also be used (Figure 11-9).

STEP 4 With a ⁵⁄₁₆″-18 bolt in the pivot hole and carrier rotate the fence to its zero position. Scribe the window from the horizontal member onto the carrier.

STEP 5 Rout away or saw out the window on the carrier.

FENCE REINFORCEMENT

The fence is 5⅞″ high so you can work stock on edge without added support. The T design is somewhat resistant to deflection. If you find the fence squirms or bends, you may want to use some form of reinforcement (Figure 11-10). Wooden corner braces or metal L brackets in aluminum or steel are good choices. I used ⁵⁄₁₆″ thick 1¾″ × 2¾″ × 4″ long right-angle aluminum. The stuff is not really square even if new, so you may have to machine it square.

VACUUM ACCESSORIES

I made a rough manifold for my vacuum from scrap ½″ plastic, a piece of wood and a chrome-plated 1½″ brass sink drain pipe (Figure 11-11). As romantic and perhaps heroic, as that may be, I recommend you buy some ready-made attachments from suppliers mentioned in this book.

Figure 11-11

My exhaust manifold is a lot of work. I think the molded plastic ones are cheaper and perhaps better.

USING THE FINE (MICRO) ADJUST

A pivot mechanism is an excellent way to position the fence either continuously or incrementally. I use a ¼"-20 screw to move the fence at the pivot arm point, a rather coarse adjustment (about ³⁄₆₄" per rotation), but the fence movement at its center, by the bit, is half the distance—only ³⁄₁₂₈" per rotation. There is no connection between the screw and the fence. The screw end simply butts up against the edge of the fence. (A flathead screw is installed in the horizontal member where the lead screw contacts to keep the wood from wearing.) I use a clamp lever and pad (washer) to lock the fence, and when I adjust the fence away from the cutter I loosen the lock just enough so there is some resistance to the advancement of the screw. On the return trip I have to push the fence against the screw. (Clamp lever KHB-64 and pad JFF-19305, Reid Tool Supply, (800) 367-8056, Muskegon, Michigan.)

The Lead Screw

The lead (travel) screw is simply a ¼"-20 threaded rod or bolt with a knob attached (Reid Tool, DK-32). The rod is 6" long and resides in two ¼"-20 steel threaded cross dowels (Part #CD05, Bruss Fasteners, P.O. Box 88307, Grand Rapids, MI 49518-0307, (800) 536-0009). The cross dowels are situated in line (perpendicular to the centerline of the lead screw pad) with the screw pad on 3" centers in the carrier (Figure 11-12). You may have to drill out the threads in the cross dowel nearest the pad if the threads in the dowels are out of phase with each other.

Figure 11-12
My lead screw assembly is about as simple as it gets. The steel dowels just sit in their holes—what could be easier?

POSITIONING THE FENCE

Positioning the fence can be achieved by merely clamping the fence in place and then pivoting as necessary. If you slotted the carrier, you'll need to install some T-nuts in your table top for two ⁵⁄₁₆"-18 bolts, which slide through and in the slots. These are really clamp bolts.

STEP 1   Position and center the carrier on the table so its most forward position covers the cutter hole in the top and clamp in place.

STEP 2   Punch or otherwise mark the back end of the slot (Figure 11-13) for the access holes to the T-nuts.

STEP 3   Drill for one set of the T-nuts and every 2-³⁄₈" for as many nuts as you'd like. I used two sets. The nuts, of course, must all be in line and on the same centers as the slots in the carrier.

STEP 4   Make a ¾"×1¼"×22" long maple washer for the ⁵⁄₁₆" clamp bolts (Figure 11-14).

Figure 11-13
Mark through the rear end of the slots for the T-nut location.

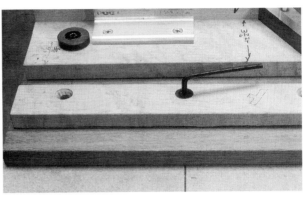

Figure 11-14
I also use this maple washer as the fence on my bench beam. Nevertheless, it has worked very well, and without it you'd mar-up the carrier in no time.

USING THE FENCE

The fence is wide enough for stock up to 10″ to 12″ wide to be worked on its edge. Material standing on end will require further support, but if you can't easily table rout it, you should consider hand routing or using another tool. My fence is narrow enough so if it changes shape I can joint it on my 6″ jointer. Most of the cuts I do require less than a ½″ of fence adjustment. So I first rough position near the centerline of the cutter hole and clamp the carrier in place. Usu-ally I have the pivot in the center of adjustment so I can pivot plus or minus from the center of travel (Figure 11-15). If you'd like to move the fence by increment, lock the fence and open the screw. Place a known thickness spacer between the fence and the screw. Rotate the fence against the screw (Figure 11-16). The fence travel will be very close to half the thickness of the spacer. That is, if I use a ¼″ drill bit as a spacer between the end of the screw and the screw pad, the ad-justment is ⅛″.

Figure 11-15
Note the equal amount of lead screw thread on both sides of the cross dowel. There is more adjustment latitude when the fence is in the center of travel.

Figure 11-16
Here I've inserted a ½″ transfer punch between the fence and the lead screw. The fence will have traveled ¼″ at the cutter centerline.

CHAPTER TWELVE
Typical Table and Hand Routing Procedures

The router and its array of jigs, fixtures, accessories and cutters presents an awesome spectrum of capability. No other tool has quite the range of its application, and indeed some processes simply can't be done with any other tool. Just because the router is so adept at solving problems and is able to find its way into so many woodworking habitats, it doesn't necessarily follow that it should be good at everything it does. For example planing, rounding spheres, deep dovetail work and timber frame joinery are all possible with a router—but not necessarily very practical with one. The router does bring these processes into our grasp, however, where they would otherwise be left only to heavy industry or those with very high level hand skills.

In this chapter I'd like to present a few of the procedures that are well within the routing province and represent the correct balance of work performed vs. the output capacity. To put it in terms of athletics, it is as if a runner trained for marathons, truly the ultimate capacity, ran only 10-kilometer races.

Figure 12-1
This double tongue and groove takes five setup changes but only one cutter: a ¼" slotter. The material is 2½" thick.

THE TONGUE AND GROOVE (EDGE TO EDGE)

The hallmark of a router task well matched to its responsibility is the quality and consistency of its cut. Another measure of appropriateness is the range of capacity within that responsibility and the degree of imposed stress. Some cutters and jigs are so job specific and work within such a narrow range of conditions that they are useless for general work; not so with the router-cut tongue and groove. Not only is the T & G router joint easy and fast to make, but with just two cheap cutters a surprising run of conditions are possible.

With a ¼″ slotter and ¾″ diameter straight bit, cuts to ½″ wide on stock up to 1½″ thick are possible without much ado. Moreover, there is little cutter wear or stress on the motor. Cuts on thicker stock, however, do require more passes through and by the cutters and more setup adjustments. Nevertheless good cuttings are possible in material to about 2½″ in thickness without appreciable heroics (Figure 12-1).

The procedure I use requires no measuring tools and works on the principle of symmetry. The depths of cut are fixed, and working the stock on each face automatically centers the joint. The microadjustable fence is indispensable in setting the widths of cut, while the vertical depth of cut is critical only to the second cutting procedure, whether slot or tongue.

Let's do an ordinary table cut on 1″ thick material. The material has to be of uniform thickness and edge jointed for the process. A ³⁄₁₆″-wide tongue and slot are quite acceptable and typically the thickness of the tongue is about one-third the thickness of the stock.

The Tongue

STEP 1   Collet up a ¾″ straight bit such as a CMT 811-690. The choice of cutter is not critical, but use a cutter whose cutting diameter is at least ⅝″ but less than 1″ in flute length.

STEP 2   "Eyeball" adjust the cutter height to one-third the thickness of stock, in this case approximately ¹¹⁄₃₂″ (Figure 12-2).

STEP 3   Now adjust the fence to allow about ³⁄₁₆″ of cutter extension and test on scrap if you'd like (Figure 12-3).

STEP 4   Cut a rabbet on both faces of the stock, thereby producing a centered tongue (Figure 12-4).

Figure 12-2
Adjust the cutter to about one-third of the stock thickness.

Figure 12-3
Eyeball the fence and cutter for an approximate ³⁄₁₆″ cut. A cut on scrap confirms the setup.

Figure 12-4
Cut a rabbet with one face down on the top then flip it over and cut another one. A lot of joinery can be simplified by this auto-centering technique.

Figure 12-5

Line up the bottom of a slotter tooth with the bottom of the tongue.

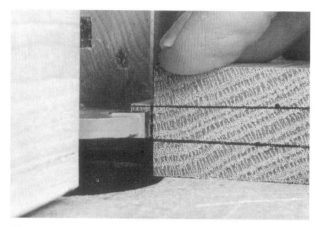

Figure 12-6

Rotate the cutter so one of its teeth is at 6 o'clock. Line it up to a scribe line across the base of the tongue.

Figure 12-7

The slot for this cut is less than ½", therefore one ¼" slotter can produce the cut without a depth of cut change. In this second pass you can see the cutter is taking less than a ¼" slot.

The Slot

STEP 1   Collet up a ¼" slotter (without a bearing) such as CMT 822-364B.

STEP 2   Eyeball the cutter height so the bottom of a tooth is even with the bottom of the tongue (Figure 12-5).

STEP 3   Adjust the fence to less than ³⁄₁₆" of cutter projection. You can use the pre-cut tongue as a guide (Figure 12-6).

STEP 4   Now slot (on equal-thickness scrap material) the workpiece, working on both faces of the stock. The cut is automatically centered (Figure 12-7).

STEP 5   Test the fit in thickness. If it's a "hammer" fit it's too tight, if it rattles it's too loose. Adjust the cutter height up or down for a "slip" fit—no rattles, no hammering. Repeat on scrap.

STEP 6   Adjust the fence so the slot is slightly deeper than the tongue is wide (Figure 12-8). The ideal amount of slop is .002" to .004". This completes the joint.

THE DOVETAIL SLOT FOR LEGS AND STILES (ROUTER TABLE)

A dovetail leg and rail connection is a wonderful connection for tables, chairs and some cabinets. The best approach to the joint is to cut only a single cutter-width dovetail tunnel. Adjusting the fit for a dovetail connection is difficult, and if the tunnel width is more than one cutter width the cutting process is quite burdensome. Dovetail bits are relatively cheap ($10 to $25), so when I design a joint I choose a bit that is most appropriate for the tenon (Figure 12-9). If I don't have the cutter, I'll buy the one I need.

Dovetail bits can only be used at one vertical

Figure 12-8A
Test the fit in thickness. Note how the tongue fits in thickness but the slot is deliberately too shallow.

Figure 12-8B
Make a fence adjustment so the slot is slightly deeper than the tongue. The depths are just right in this sample: .002″ to .004″ slop is just enough room for excess glue.

Figure 12-9
The socket for this tenon was cut to just one cutter width. The tenon then is the same size as the cutter. The neck at the base of the tenon should be about one-third or more the thickness of the stock.

depth of cut because any change in depth will spoil the preceding profile. A full cutter width and one full cutter depth then is all that is permissible. A long dovetail bit cut to full depth in one pass will break the cutter at the shank. A straight bit pre-plowing is essential before the dovetail bit can be introduced. So while you're selecting the dovetail bit, find a straight bit that is as long as the required depth of cut and narrower than any section of the dovetail (Figure 12-10). The straight bit cut, in all likelihood, will need to be cut at several depths. Deep, single-pass slots with a straight bit can break the bit. Underlaying the workpiece with ¼″-thick layers of MDF or plastic will make the depth changes easy. The procedure is as follows:

STEP 1 Collet up the appropriate straight bit and set it to the dovetail depth less ¹⁄₁₆″ (Figure 12-11).

STEP 2 Stack up as many layers of ¼″ material to equal the depth of cut less ¼″ (Figure 12-12).

STEP 3 Set up a length stop to limit the workpiece travel. Allow about ⅛″ of extra travel (Figure 12-13). When the dovetail is cut you should back up the stop so the workpiece travel is shorter by ⅛″. If this is not done the dovetail bit will take a full bite at the end of the tunnel and it could break there.

STEP 4 Slide workpieces down the fence, over the cutter and against the stop, removing an underlayer for each new depth of cut. Don't spend any time at the end of the slot or you'll burn the stock and dull the cutter (Figure 12-14).

Figure 12-10

This straight bit is smaller in diameter than the dovetail cutter behind it. Sometimes I'll take the cut in three stages: first a straight bit, then a small dovetail bit, followed with the final but larger dovetail cutter.

Figure 12-11

The dovetail cut will be ¾" deep. I've set this straight bit to cut to ¹¹/₁₆".

Figure 12-12

Here I only need two ¼"-thick layers of plastic to raise the workpiece. The first depth of cut will be ³/₁₆" (¹¹/₁₆"–⁸/₁₆" = ³/₁₆").

STEP 5   After all the slots (open mortises) are cut, collet up the dovetail cutter and set to full depth (Figure 12-15).

STEP 6   Don't move the fence or the dovetail will be on a different center than the slot. Test the first dovetail slot on a piece of scrap that has had the same treatment (slotting) as your finished stock. The dovetail cut is similar in dynamics to most straight cuts, but it's wise to preview the control and handling on scrap.

STEP 7   Back the stop up by ⅛" and cut all the dovetails at full depth (Figure 12-16). Hold the stock firmly against the fence and down on the table. If the stock is

poorly dimensioned it may not steer straight down the fence or it may rock. The dovetail bit is fully engaged now and any deviation may ruin the slot or kick back the workpiece. On square stock, pay particular attention to how square the fence is to the table (Figure 12-17). Any deviation will compound your handling problems.

A DOVETAIL TENON (HAND ROUTED)

A dovetail tenon is best cut with an offset sub-base and the hand router. The bench beam, a

Figure 12-13

The length of workpiece travel for the straight bit should be about ⅛″ further than the path of the dove-tail cutter. I'll slide the stop to the right ⅛″ after I've cut all the slots.

Figure 12-14

Since the cutter is initially set to full depth, chatter, "stepping" and similar defects are absent from the profile. You must hold the stock firmly, however, as any deviation will spoil the cut.

right-angle template and a collar are also required. This procedure is for a two-faced tenon. You may wish to hand cut a third face or shoulder on one end of the tenon so the bottom of the way (the dovetail slot) is covered.

The process is a cut-and-fit reiteration procedure. There is simply no way to pre-adjust the guide and depth of cut for a perfect fit on the first cut. The workpiece has to be reversed in the fixture for the opposite face of the cut and for symmetry. A right-angle template can be fashioned from a 10″ to 12″ long by 7″ to 9″ wide piece of ⅜″ or ½″ MDF. A cleat beneath the

Figure 12-15

The dovetail bit will clear a pathway larger than the straight bit and about ¹⁄₁₆″ deeper.

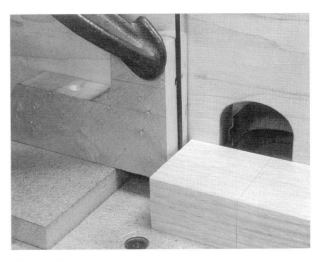

Figure 12-16

Move the stop ⅛″ to the right. A ⅛″ transfer punch between the stop and the workpiece will facilitate the repositioning.

Figure 12-17

The fence should be square to the work surface for all cuts, but it is especially critical on this final pass.

template must be situated so the work edge of the template is at right angles to it (Figure 12-18). A Porter Cable collar guide #42021 will accept any dovetail bit, and since it is ⁷⁄₁₆″ in length it can be used on ½″-thick template material.

Cutting a Dovetail Tenon

STEP 1   Prepare your stock and cut some spare material for the calibration cuts.

STEP 2   Locate and index the workpiece up against the overhanging template (Figure 12-19). *Note*: Since the socket (the dovetail tunnel) is one cutter width, the dovetail tenon will be the same size as the cutter. Since we know this, we can approximate the depths and template positions with some reference to size.

STEP 3   Collet up the same dovetail cutter used to make the tunnel and set its projec-

Figure 12-18

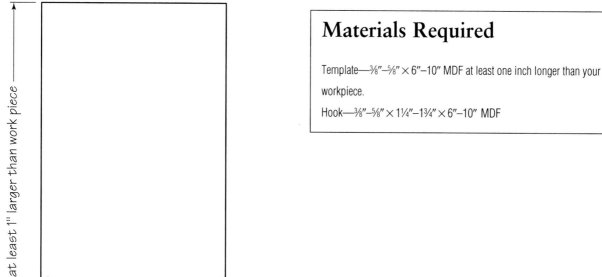

Materials Required

Template—⅜″–⅝″ × 6″–10″ MDF at least one inch longer than your workpiece.
Hook—⅜″–⅝″ × 1¼″–1¾″ × 6″–10″ MDF

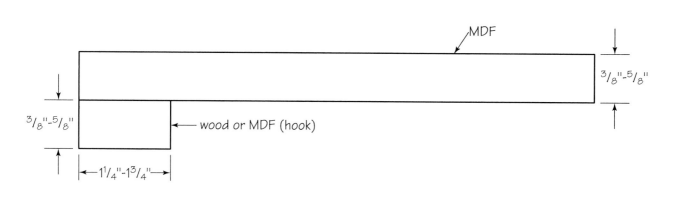

tion to equal the depth of the tunnel plus the thickness of the template. Use a PC 42021 collar guide or any collar guide that will allow the cutter entry (Figure 12-20).

STEP 4 Now position the template for your first approximation and clamp it down. Pass the router along the template and eyeball the cutter pathway (power off). On this first cut I usually produce a shoulder I know is too short. A climb cut is permissible here, especially if the cut is a light cut. If you have any apprehension, then anti-climb cut (Figure 12-21).

STEP 5 Reverse the workpiece and repeat the cut, indexing as before (Figure 12-22).

STEP 6 Now test the tenon in the way (the tunnel). Adjust the depth of cut if necessary. The best depth of cut is equal to the tunnel depth less about .003″ to .005″ (the thickness of a dollar bill). If the tenon is too wide, slide the template over about half the distance of

Figure 12-20
I've got the machine upside down here. With the template and the socket workpiece I can make the first approximation of the depth of cut.

Figure 12-21
A reasonable first approximation of the shoulder cut is one where at least some of the bottom of the cutter is engaged in the workpiece.

Figure 12-19
The fence on my bench beam is square to the work surface. A workpiece against the fence and up against the template is indexed and ready for the cut.

Figure 12-22
The second pass on the opposite face of the stock centers the cut.

the misfit. (If it's ¼″ too wide move the template ⅛″.)

STEP 7   Play both depths of cut on scrap until you achieve a slip fit—no hammering and no rattling. When the test fit is acceptable, cut the two faces on all your stock.

STEP 8   A third shoulder can be cut across the end. You must reposition the template (Figure 12-23). A cut straight across the template will produce a straight shoulder. The end of the tunnel is a radius of the cutter, so it won't be a perfect fit. A specialized template with a rounded projection can produce the exact fit, but it'll take some time and practice to make right (Figure 12-24).

A FULL-THICKNESS PATTERN CUT (HAND ROUTED)

There are dozens of pattern cutters for cutting both templates and woodwork (Figure 12-25). The nicest way to cut a workpiece to the size of the template is to use a pattern bit with a bearing on the shank. A cutter of this sort requires the template on top of the workpiece. In this configuration the template is much easier to position and clamp. A full-thickness cut often requires 2 to 3 hp. An occasional cut can be done with a 1⅛″- hp tool, but all-day cuttings should be done with a 3 hp router or a shaper if the stock is 1¼″ thick or thicker. Outside single-depth cuttings should also be done with a fixed-base router. Three of the best tool bits for flush template work include the PRC 818-C-GR (1¼″ flute length), the CMT 811-690B (1″ flute) and the CMT 812-690B (1½″ flute). You must balance the template thickness, flute length and

Figure 12-23
I've repositioned the template so I can make the third shoulder of the tenon.

Figure 12-24
This is a sample of a template that, when used with a bearing-guided cutter, can produce a rounded third shoulder like the one shown. It's no easy task to get a perfect match.

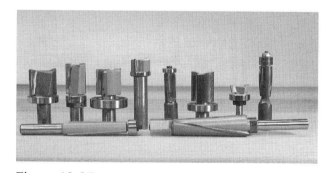

Figure 12-25
I do a lot of pattern work so I have a lot of pattern bits. The largest (shown without bearing) is made by PRC and has a 2½″ flute length. Pattern bits have shank bearings and bearings on the end of the tool. The O.D. of the bearing needn't be the same diameter as the cutter but it shouldn't be less.

Figure 12-26
To minimize the chance of an accident or an accidental cut, balance the flute length, template thickness and workpiece thickness so no more than ⅛" of the cutter extends beyond the work. This excessive flute length is dangerous.

thickness of work so that a minimum of cutter extends beyond the workpiece (Figure 12-26).

A template cut straight down the long grain is a fairly safe and easy cut to make. It's when the pattern weaves back and forth or cuts across grain that you should be concerned. A cutter advancing into and out of end grain is met with an ever-changing resistance and work load. That means your hand feed will also be met with ever-changing and unpredictable forces and speed. Be aware that in routings such as these, you'll need good footing and secure clamping.

Full Thickness Pattern Cutting

STEP 1 Mark the pattern on the workpiece with a washer or spacer so that your scribeline is ⅟₁₆" to ⅛" larger than the template (Figure 12-27). Also mark the net size of the template so you can relocate it easier.

STEP 2 Now band saw or jigsaw off the waste.

STEP 3 Secure the template to the workpiece (Figure 12-28). For ordinary work, clamping is all that's required. If the cut is occasional but critical you may want to screw the template to the

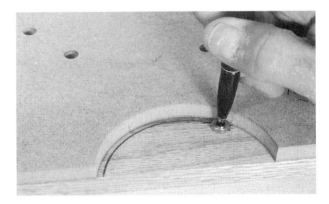

Figure 12-27
Mark (scribe) the pattern on the workpiece about ⅟₁₆" or so from the edge of the template.

Figure 12-28
Use at least two clamps on the template and the workpiece. One clamp on the workpiece and in the same place on the template counts as one clamp on each.

Figure 12-29

Pattern work is demanding, high-powered routing. Use a cutter at least ¾" in diameter and adjust its extension to a minimum. If you cannot safely match the length to thickness, consider using a collar guide.

Figure 12-30

With thin material like this I can safely climb cut along the grain. If the cuttings are wavy or cross-grained, a climb cut could be dangerous. If in doubt, anti-climb cut!

work. If the cut is a production cut, consider a vacuum template. Avoid a router mat or double-sided tape.

STEP 4   Collet up the shortest cutter for the job and adjust the depth of cut to the full thickness plus ¹⁄₃₂" to ¹⁄₁₆" (Figure 12-29).

STEP 5   Rout anti-climb in end grain; if the overhang is minimal, climb cutting on long grain is permissible, at some risk (Figure 12-30).

DECORATIVE SLOTTING

Shallow, narrow slotting is an interesting method of decoration. These simple router table cuttings are restricted to straight, flat workpieces like legs, rails, stiles or drawer fronts. The effect is not unlike that of Art Deco designs. It's easy to do and adds a nice touch to an otherwise mundane piece (Figure 12-31).

The process requires only a slotter and its arbor (Figure 12-32). Because the arbors are relatively short, the reach of the slotter is limited to about an 1½" from the edge of stock. That is equivalent to the center of a 3"-wide workpiece, however. The process is simplified by the use of symmetry. Make one cut and before changing the depth of cut flip the work over so all the

Figure 12-31

The legs on my pin router stand were decorated with a ¹⁄₁₆" slotter. It's a goofy thing to do, but where's the harm? It gives me a chance to preview "the look," so I know what I'm getting into on a custom piece.

cuts will be spaced equally from the centerline. WKW makes the thinnest cutter I know of (.050″), but I suspect you can have a thinner one made. Slots near .050″ × .050″ have about the right amount of shadow for me, so set the fence for a .050″ extension of the cutter if you agree. I like a spacing of about an ⅛″ between stripes. A cut this shallow can be climb cut if desired, but the workpiece still can self-feed if you lose it.

Routing For .050″ Square Slots on .175″ Centers

STEP 1 Collet up the slotter and adjust the fence. Decide whether you want to work from the edge or the center. In either case you may want to use spacers under the workpiece to adjust the depth (Figure 12-33).

STEP 2 Pass the work by the cutter and then flip the part over for the second cut.

STEP 3 Change the depth of cut by .175″ (about ³⁄₁₆″) and repeat as desired.

Figure 12-32
This WKW slotter is the thinnest tool I know of (above). It's fragile and can bend, so use flat, straight, well jointed stock with it.

Figure 12-33A&B
I'm slotting from the center to the edge. I found some plastic just the right thickness for the spaces I want. I pull one spacer out after each pair of cuts. This would take forever with a hand router.

EDGE JOINTING ON THE ROUTER TABLE

The very high speed of router bits and the fact that carbide is readily available make router jointing competitive with the jointer. The process is, however, restricted to the edges of stock, since a long unsupported cutter is not possible with ordinary routers. There are advantages to router jointing besides the crisp square edges. A carbide cutter means you can joint plywood, plastic, MDF, particle board and even wood, of all things. There are virtually no knife setup hassles as there are with a jointer. A regrind for a straight bit costs no more than $5 in most cases; compare that with jointer blades at 50 cents, or more, per inch of blade.

Once again the jointing capabilities are restricted to the edges of less than 8/4 stock. There is only one possible feed direction, anti-climb (right to left), and the depth of cut should be less than 1/16". The cutter height should be adjusted to less than 1/16" above the stock, and large-diameter carbide straight bits are the cutters of choice. The jointing system can be arranged on any fence, but is particularly easy to zero out with the microadjust fence.

Jointing On The Router Table

STEP 1   Collet up a straight bit (at least 3/4" in cutting diameter) and adjust its height to about 1/16" over the work thickness (Figure 12-34).

STEP 2   Select some sheet stock (aluminum, brass or Formica) of a thickness from .010" to .060" and clamp it to the outfeed (left) side of the fence (Figure 12-35). Whatever thickness you choose will be the depth of cut.

Figure 12-34

Adjust the cutter height to match the thickness of the work. Allow no more extension than you might want rabbetted into your flesh—for me that's about 1/64".

Figure 12-35

I use a thin piece of cabinet liner Formica (thickness .018") to offset the outfeed side of the fence. It doesn't seem like much, but most ordinary stock cleans up in less than three passes.

STEP 3 Now adjust the cutting circle of the cutter tangent to the outfeed face of the fence (Figure 12-36).

STEP 4 Check for tangency with a prejointed stick. Joint the first 2″ of the stick and stop the motor. If the stick hits the spacer (Formica in my case), back the fence up a quarter turn or so and rejoint. If there is space between the spacer and the stock add a quarter turn or so of fence (Figure 12-37) and so on until the workpiece slides without overcutting or bumping into the spacer. A new cutter will probably joint fifty to a hundred 6′ edges of stock before sharpening is needed. Light cuts with well-matched feed rates will prolong the cutter life. I made a 42″-long dedicated router jointer that joints better than my iron-horse jointer by far. I've jointed stuff within .002″ on stock over 6′ long, and it's a joy to use.

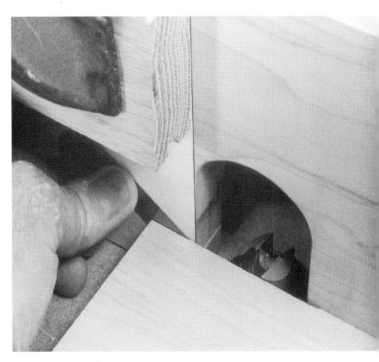

Figure 12-37A
This .005″ feeler gauge fits between the work and the fence. This is an overcut.

Figure 12-36
The highest point in the cutting circle rotation should be tangent to the outfeed side of the fence. Use a straightedge and the microadjust fence to set the tangency.

Figure 12-37B
The work runs into the fence in this view, so not enough stock has been jointed. Move the fence back so the work just clears the Formica. Test this adjustment on a pre-jointed straight stick for best results.

LIST OF SUPPLIERS

Bridge City Tool Works
1104 N.E. 28th Ave.
Portland, OR 97232
(800) 253-3332
Precision layout and metrology
tools.

Bruss Fasteners
P.O. Box 88307
Grand Rapids, MI 49518-0307
(800) 563-0009
Hardware, T-nuts, screws,
x-dowels and other specialty
fasteners.

Cascade Tools, Inc.
P.O. Box 3110
Bellingham, WA 98227
Huge selection of Taiwanese
made router bits.

CMT Tools
310 Mears Blvd.
Oldsmar, FL 34677
(813) 891-6160
Premiere router bits and router
offset subbases.

DeWalt Industrial Tool Co.
P.O. Box 158
625 Hanover Pike
Hampstead, MD 21074
(800) 4-DeWalt
Electric hand tools.

Eagle America
P.O. Box 1099
Chardon, OH 44024
One of the largest router bit se-
lections in North America.

Garrett Wade Co.
161 Avenue of the Americas
New York, NY 10013
(800) 221-2942
Subbases and thousands of
other quality tools.

Magnate Business International
1930 S. Brea Canyon Rd.
Diamond Bar, CA 91765
(909) 861-1185
Router bits and offset subbases.

Microfence
11100 Cumpston St. #35
North Hollywood, CA 91601
(800) 480-6427
Nicely adjustable edge guides
and circle-cutter pivots for most
routers.

Paso Robles Carbide, Inc.
731-C Paso Robles St.
Paso Robles, CA 93446
(805) 238-6144
Router bits, many of the long-
est, largest diameter and other
parameters on the extreme end.

Patrick Warner
1427 Kenora St.
Escondido, CA 92027
(619) 747-2623 or FAX (619)
745-1753
Maker and supplier of acrylic
offset router bases.

Patrick Spielman
Spielman's Woodworks
3771 Gibraltar Rd.
Fish Creek, WI 54212
(414) 868-3488
The "Encyclopedia" of routing.

Porter Cable Corp.
P.O. Box 2468
Jackson, TN 38302
(901) 668-8600
Routers, router accessories and
other electric hand tools.

Reid Tool Supply Co.
2265 Black Creek Rd.
Muskegon, MI 49444-2684
(800) 253-0421
Jig and fixture hardware of all
sorts.

Ridge Carbide Tool Co.
595 New York Ave.
Lyndhurst, NJ 07071
(800) 443-0992
Sharpening of router bits.

The L.S. Starrett Co.
121 Crescent St.
Athol, MA 01331
Precision scales, calipers and layout tools, etc.

Wisconsin Knife Works
2505 Kennedy Dr.
Beloit, WI 53511
(608) 363-7888
Plunging and other router bits.

Woolcraft, Inc.
P.O. Box 687
1222 W. Ardmore Ave.
Itasca, IL 60143
(708) 773-4777
Supply a nice spring clamp for
temporary hold fast.

Woodhaven
5323 W. Kimberly Rd.
Davenport, IA 52806
(800) 344-6657
Routing equipment.

Woodwork
P.O. Box 1529
Ross, CA 94957-9987
A magazine for all
woodworkers.

INDEX

METRIC CONVERSION CHART		
TO CONVERT	TO	MULTIPLY BY
Inches	Centimeters	2.54
Centimeters	Inches	0.4
Feet	Centimeters	30.5
Centimeters	Feet	0.03
Yards	Meters	0.9
Meters	Yards	1.1
Sq. Inches	Sq. Centimeters	6.45
Sq. Centimeters	Sq. Inches	0.16
Sq. Feet	Sq. Meters	0.09
Sq. Meters	Sq. Feet	10.8
Sq. Yards	Sq. Meters	0.8
Sq. Meters	Sq. Yards	1.2
Pounds	Kilograms	0.45
Kilograms	Pounds	2.2
Ounces	Grams	28.4
Grams	Ounces	0.04

More Great Books for Your Woodshop!

Measure Twice, Cut Once, Revised Edition—Miscalculation will be a thing of the past when you learn these effective techniques for checking and adjusting measuring tools, laying out complex measurements, fixing mistakes, making templates and much more! *#70330/$22.99/144 pages/144 color illus.*

100 Keys to Woodshop Safety—Make your shop safer than ever with this manual designed to help you avoid potential pitfalls. Tips and illustrations demonstrate the basics of safe shopwork—from using electricity safely and avoiding trouble with hand and power tools to ridding your shop of dangerous debris and handling finishing materials. *#70333/$17.99/64 pages/125 color illus.*

Making Elegant Gifts from Wood—Develop your woodworking skills and make over 30 gift-quality projects at the same time! You'll find everything you're looking to create in your gifts—variety, timeless styles, pleasing proportions and imaginative designs that call for the best woods. Plus, technique sidebars and hardware installation tips make your job even easier. *#70331/ $24.99/128 pages/30 color, 120 b&w illus.*

Good Wood Handbook, Second Edition—Now you can select and use the right wood for the job—before you buy. You'll discover valuable information on a wide selection of commercial softwoods and hardwoods—from common uses, color and grain to how the wood glues and takes finish. *#70329/$19.99/128 pages/250 color illus.*

100 Keys to Preventing & Fixing Woodworking Mistakes—Stop those mistakes before they happen—and fix those that have already occurred. Numbered tips and color illustrations show you how to work around flaws in wood; fix mistakes made with the saw, plane, router and lathe; repair badly made joints, veneering mishaps and finishing blunders; assemble projects successfully and more! *#70332/$17.99/64 pages/ 125 color illus.*

Build Your Own Mobile Power Tool Centers—Learn how to "expand" shop space by building mobile workstations that maximize utility, versatility and accessibility of woodshop tools and accessories. *#70283/$19.99/144 pages/ 250 b&w illus./paperback*

Creating Your Own Woodshop—Discover dozens of economical ways to fill unused space with the woodshop of your dreams. Self shows you how to convert space, lay out the ideal woodshop, or improve your existing shop. *#70229/ $18.99/128 pages/162 b&w photos/illus./paperback*

Tables You Can Customize—Learn how to build four types of basic tables—from a Shaker coffee table to a Stickley library table— then discover how to apply a wide range of variations to customize the pieces to fit your personal needs. *#70299/$19.99/128 pages/150 b&w illus./paperback*

How To Sharpen Every Blade in Your Woodshop—You know that tools perform best when razor sharp—yet you avoid the dreaded chore. This ingenious guide brings you plans for jigs and devices that make sharpening any blade short and simple! Includes jigs for sharpening boring tools, router bits and more! *#70250/$17.99/144 pages/157 b&w illus./paperback*

The Woodworker's Sourcebook, 2nd Edition—Shop for woodworking supplies from home! Self has compiled listings for everything from books and videos to plans and associations. Each listing has an address and telephone number and is rated in terms of quality and price. *#70281/$19.99/160 pages/50 illus.*

Basic Woodturning Techniques—Detailed explanations of fundamental techniques like faceplate and spindle turning will have you turning beautiful pieces in no time. *#70211/$14.95/112 pages/119 b&w illus./paperback*

The Stanley Book of Woodworking Tools, Techniques and Projects—Become a better woodworker by mastering the fundamentals of choosing the right wood, cutting tight-fitting joints, properly using a marking gauge and much more. *#70264/$19.95/160 pages/400 color illus./ paperback*

Good Wood Routers—Get the most from your router with this comprehensive guide to hand-held power routers and table routing. You'll discover a world of information about types of routers, their uses, maintenance, setup, precision table routing and much, much more. *#70319/$19.99/128 pages/550 color illus.*

Tune Up Your Tools—Bring your tools back to perfect working order and experience safe, accurate cutting, drilling and sanding. With this handy reference you'll discover how to tune up popular woodworking machines, instructions for aligning your tools, troubleshooting charts and many other tips. *#70308/$22.99/144 pages/150 b&w illus./paperback*

Desks You Can Customize—Customize your furniture to fit your personal style. With Graves's instruction and detailed drawings, you'll create a unique, individualized desk as you experiment with legs, doors, drawers, organizers and much

more. *#70309/$19.99/128 pages/133 b&w illus./ paperback*

Make Your Woodworking Pay for Itself, Revised Edition—Find simple hints for selling your work to generate a little extra income! You'll find hints on easy ways to save on wood and tools, ideas for projects to sell, guidance for handling money and more! Plus, new information on home-business zoning and tax facts keeps you up-to-date. *#70320/$18.99/128 pages/20 b&w illus./paperback*

Marvelous Wooden Boxes You Can Make—Master woodworker Jeff Greef offers plans for 20 beautiful, functional boxes, complete with drawings, cutting lists, numbered step-by-step instructions and color photographs. *#70287/ $24.99/144 pages/67 color, 225 b&w illus.*

Good Wood Joints—Learn which joints are best for specific situations and how to skillfully make them. You'll discover joints for every application, the basics of joint cutting and much more! Plus, you'll find an ingenious chart that makes choosing the right joint for the job easy. All well-illustrated with step-by-step instructions for making joinery by machine or hand. *#70313/$19.99/ 128 pages/550 color illus.*

Woodworker's Guide to Pricing Your Work—Turn your hobby into profit! You'll find out how other woodworkers set their prices and sell their products. You'll learn how to estimate average materials cost per project, increase your income without sacrificing quality or enjoyment, build repeat and referral business, manage a budget and much more! *#70268/$18.99/160 pages/paperback*

Display Cabinets You Can Customize—Go beyond building to designing furniture. You'll receive step-by-step instructions to the base projects—the starting points for a wide variety of pieces, such as display cabinets, tables and cases. Then you'll learn about customizing techniques. You'll see how to adapt a glass-front cabinet; put a profile on a cabinet by using molding; get a different look by using stained glass or changing the legs; and much more! *#70282/$18.99/128 pages/150 b&w illus./paperback*